How to Order:
Single copies of this book may be ordered from Prima
Publishing, P.O. Box 1260BK, Rocklin, CA 95677; telephone
(916) 632-4400. Quantity discounts are also available. On
your letterhead, include information concerning the intended use of the books and the number of books you wish
to purchase.

....

How to
Test and Improve
Your Own
Mental Health

....

George D. Cohen, LCSW
William Gladstone, M.A.

Prima Publishing
P.O. Box 1260BK
Rocklin, CA 95677
(916) 632-4400

Production by Robin Lockwood
Copyediting by Darlene Bledsoe
Composition by WESType Publishing Services, Inc.
Interior design by Renee Deprey
Cover design by Page Design, Inc.

Library of Congress Cataloging-in-Publication Data

Cohen, George D.
  How to test and improve your own mental health / George D. Cohen, William Gladstone.
      p.   cm.
  Includes bibliographical references and index.
  ISBN 1-55958-555-2
  1. Mental health. 2. Mental illness. 3. Mental health—Testing.
I. Gladstone, William. II. Title.
RA790.C668   1994
616.89—dc20   94-27376
                                                              CIP

95 96 97 98 99 RRD 10 9 8 7 6 5 4 3 2 1

Printed in the United States of America

Contents

Acknowledgments

The authors would like to acknowledge the contributions of the many mental health professionals who made this book possible. First, we would like to thank Dr. Douglas H. Powell of Harvard University Health Services. Dr. Powell developed the Theory of the Five Stages of Adaptability in conjunction with his research as a NASA consultant and Harvard University-affiliated psychologist. His concepts are part of a general theory of personality and normal behavior that he has subsequently developed in his own work.

We were sufficiently inspired by Dr. Powell's work to create our own Test of Adaptability. Furthermore, we have adapted Dr. Powell's theory to the needs of the general public and have developed our own thoughts concerning the nature and treatment of mental illness and emotional well-being. The Test of Adaptability and the remainder of this book are entirely the responsibility of the authors.

We would also like to thank the many other researchers, psychologists, and psychiatrists who have generously allowed their tests to be adapted and reproduced for this book. We are grateful for their skill, dedication, and diligence in devising practical testing instruments for the benefit of all.

Finally, we have relied on our own backgrounds and experience as a clinical psychotherapist and a professional anthropologist in presenting this material in a sensitive and useful manner. In putting together our unique package of tests and information, we have attempted to be faithful to the spirit of the material we have selected.

A NOTE OF THANKS

To Diane Hill for her support, patience, and excellent editorial assistance.

To Janice Shuffield and the staff of Waterside Productions for their generous support and assistance.

Introduction

Now more than ever it is important to take responsibility for your own health, which includes your mental health and emotional well-being. We live in challenging times. On one hand we have a greater range of effective treatments—both medical and psychological—than ever before. On the other hand, access to all types of health care is becoming limited due to astronomically rising costs. Mental health benefits in particular are limited in managed health-care programs and as part of normal health insurance benefits. The entire health-care system is in a state of upheaval and change. Hopefully, a more accessible health-care delivery system will soon be in place.

In the midst of these contradictions and the many other stresses of modern life, we are left with a question: What can people do to protect their health and that of their families? One response is to take a positive preventative path to good health. An ounce of prevention might include a program of exercise, proper nutrition, and self-care through knowledge. Knowledge is your greatest power. Knowledge about mental health is part of an informed program of self-care. It is more important than ever that you be able to recognize the signs and symptoms of emotional health and emotional stress. We

1

need this knowledge, not only to seek help in a timely way but to find appropriate resources that are affordable. Finally, we need this information to avoid unnecessary suffering caused by false pride, fear, and lack of knowledge about mental health. Twenty percent of all Americans will experience some form of mental or emotional disorder during their lives, and only one-third of those will go for help.

In the course of a lifetime you will probably survive dozens of physical illnesses. Most will clear up spontaneously; for others you will consult a doctor. In a similar way you will also go through emotional disturbances. Many you will handle on your own, but for some you may need help. How can you know which is which?

In most cases you know whether you have a common cold or something more serious, but you're probably not so confident when it comes to emotional problems. When you experience emotional distress, you don't always know how serious the problem is or what to do about it. A medical doctor will often say, "It's just the flu. Go to bed, drink plenty of fluids, and you'll be fine in a few days." Most mental health professionals will likewise give you appropriate help, but your initial decision to seek counseling or therapy may be quite difficult to make.

This book is designed to help you learn about mental health in a very personal way. We encourage you to take the tests and to discover your own strengths and weaknesses. Take the time to share this book with friends and family. The pace of change is a challenge to all of us. We all want to get the most out of the present, but we also need to prepare ourselves for the future. We applaud your interest and courage as you test and improve your own mental health.

How to
Use This Book

Wouldn't it be great to test your mental health in the privacy of your own home or office? Wouldn't it be wonderful to put your feet up on your favorite sofa and find out about your ability to cope?

Life is certainly a great test and a great adventure. Sometimes it's smooth sailing and sometimes it's a bit overwhelming. There are times we would all like to know, How am I doing? Am I really okay? Could I be doing better? To seek self-knowledge and self-improvement are two of mankind's great motivators.

Well, now you can find the answers to these questions at your leisure. We've designed this book to make it easy and entertaining to take stock of your own mental health. Remember, you are unique and have your own particular strengths and weaknesses. Our goal is to help you get an objective picture of your own coping abilities. There is no absolute test of mental health, except perhaps the measure of your ability to survive, to thrive, and to enjoy yourself whatever your situation. Ultimately, you are your own best judge.

THE NITTY GRITTY

An important feature of this book is the table of Five Stages of Adaptability developed by psychologist Douglas H. Powell. This table consists of seven areas of human behavior (referred to as characteristics or aspects) and the expected behavior corresponding to each of the five stages of adaptability.

Our goal is to give you an accurate and positive tool for self-measurement. Our intention is to increase your clarity and understanding, and not to use labels, for their own sake. If our labels bother you, change them or throw them out, but please don't throw out the baby with the bathwater. We want you to derive the benefits that come from reading this book and taking our test.

We have provided definitions for all significant terms and a discussion with examples regarding each area of behavior. Once you are familiar with the nature of these aspects, which are significant indicators, you are ready to take the test.

You might follow these handy steps:

1. Look at the behavior patterns associated with the seven characteristics that define each stage.

2. You may take the test first, then go through the presentation of the five stages. Or, you can read about the stages and then take the test. In either case, do get a sense of each stage.

3. Check off the behavior patterns that most clearly resemble your own. Do not be surprised if some of your behavior falls into each of the five stages. Please remember that a single "disturbed trait" does not necessarily make you a disturbed person!

4. Given the subjective nature of this self-test, you are advised to take the test on at least two different occasions, which might preferably correspond to two different moods. This way you can get a more accurate reading.

5. If your first and second tests indicate that much of your behavior results from current or ongoing stress, we suggest that you might profit from some form of help. If so, please refer to Appendix C, Where to Go for Help.

Can You Adapt?

• • • •

1

••••

Adaptability: What Is It?

Roll with the punches. Go with the flow. Use it or lose it. Our daily conversations are filled with expressions that assume that the ability to be flexible and to change with the times are necessary for our health and survival. This is true whether we are talking about individual, group, national, or even corporate well-being. The concept behind these sayings is that adaptability is the key to both health and survival. Those able to adapt will prosper; those who cannot will suffer the consequences.

The idea of adaptability is really at the core of the mental health test we have created, and it is also our key concept in defining mental health. We shall use the terms "mental health" and "emotional well-being" interchangably throughout the text. Adaptability, the ability to adapt—what is it and why is it so important?

It is, first of all, the key to survival of all species of plants and animals, including humans. Charles Darwin's amazing breakthrough in the biological sciences was the observation that only species that were able to adapt to changes in their environment survived. Animals that were unable to adapt to changing conditions were simply unable to survive and were doomed to extinction. Dinosaurs are a good example of the inability to adapt.

It did not matter whether the changes were caused by the animals themselves, as in the case of overhunting, or by climatic conditions (such as the dramatic changes caused by the Ice Age), or by other animals competing for food. What matters is that after all is said and done *many animals did not adapt and did not survive.*

WHY DID HUMANS SURVIVE?

It has been said that humans survived and came to dominate the planet precisely because they remained the most adaptable of all animal species, having as their claim to fame that special organ, the human brain. We believe that as with the human species, so with human individuals. Just as Darwin believed that the health of our species lay in its ability to adapt to changing conditions, so do we suggest that individual well-being can also be viewed in terms of an individual's ability to adapt to his or her changing world. This would include all normal situations and interactions that are encountered in everyday life.

THE INFLUENCE OF CULTURE

Adaptability has a strong cultural component and may depend on where you live and even when you lived. Behavior that was adaptable in America 50 years ago may not hold true today, any more than a contemporary American definition would hold true in China or other parts of the world. Each culture, or time period, creates different modes of adaptability; the ability of an individual to adapt to a specific culture can be understood as a measure of mental health. This is a big concept because it holds true for subgroups within a given culture, and it transcends individual and group differences in values, religion, politics, or morals.

WORK, LOVE, AND PLAY

In this book we are using adaptability and mental health to imply the ability to work, love, and play in balanced measure. This definition is taken from Aristotle and the Greeks ("a sound mind in a healthy body"). Who could argue with the Greeks? Of course, there are cultures in which the behaviors associated with work, love, and play are very different from our own American society, but to our knowledge there is no society that does not value these three human capacities in some form or variety. From a *biological* point of view, some would claim that these activities are literal requirements to the continued existence of any human group (activities of production, reproduction, recuperation). In more modern times, even Sigmund Freud, the father of modern psychology, defined emotional health as the ability *to work and to love.*

INNER HARMONY

Another way of thinking about normal adaptability is to view it as living up to one's potential, whatever that potential may be. The one constant universal principle we look for is the notion of inner harmony. Consider the Chinese, whose concept of the *Tao* represents the wholeness of life. Only when men or women are at peace with themselves can their energies be directed toward adapting to their outside world, and not merely to themselves. *Umoja,* the African concept of harmony, would also extend to unity within the family, the community, and the nation. This example is one of the seven basic precepts of Kwanzaa, the annual celebration of African-American culture. Every culture in every known time period has considered harmony to be essential to human life.

WHAT IS MENTAL ILLNESS?

If mental health is defined as normal adaptation, the opposite is mental illness, which might consist of increasingly restricted patterns of adaptation, ending ultimately in the inability to adapt at all, or in death. People who are tormented by inner chaos and conflicts are unable to lend their full energies toward adapting to other people and events in the world around them. They must choose limiting patterns of interaction with others that do not demand tapping into their already overburdened resources. They are unlikely to use new response patterns and will more likely settle for dogmatic and rigid patterns of interaction with themselves and with others. These patterns will not further test or tax their limits of adaptability. The dejected and delusional painter, Vincent van Gogh, was certainly operating under severe limits when he cut off his ear lobe and gave it to a young woman. Who knows what he was really trying to express by this desperate act?

ADAPTABILITY: A MEASURING TOOL FOR MENTAL HEALTH

A fuller view of the notion of adaptability will be drawn out in more specific discussions of the different stages of adaptability. The important point we have tried to establish is that adaptability is an appropriate concept for looking at the overall picture of mental health.

The beauty of this concept is that adaptability can be *measured,* and it gives us a very practical tool for measuring mental health. In the discussion that follows, the abstract notion of adaptability has been broken down to seven concrete and observable aspects. Taken as a whole, these seven characteristics give us a very tangible picture of five stages by which humans can be distinguished, and against which their behavior can be measured.

2
• • • •

The Seven Characteristics of Human Behavior

Our model of the stages of adaptability is based on seven characteristics, or aspects:

1. Tension
2. Mood
3. Thought
4. Activity
5. Organization/Control
6. Interpersonal Relationships
7. Physical

Each aspect refers to a definable area of behavior that is distinct and observable. These are the seven characteristics that clinical psychologists have found to be useful categories in evaluating and predicting human behavior. In real life, of course, there is great interaction among these seven aspects, with changes in one characteristic often associated with and dependent upon changes in the other characteristics. For example, a change in the aspect of Mood (#2), might either provoke, or be the result of, a change in a love relationship (#6, Interpersonal). Because of their dynamic interrelationships we pay close attention to all of these seven aspects throughout this book. The five stages outlined by Dr. Powell have been defined by isolating patterns of behavior for each of the seven characteristics. When taken together as a whole, these stages and aspects indicate general levels of mental fitness.

LIKE A GOOD MYSTERY STORY

These different aspects can be compared to different kinds of evidence in a legal case or a good mystery story. A single piece of incriminating evidence, such as a motive, is not necessarily significant unless associated with other types of evidence—access to the murder weapon, lack of an alibi, opportunity to perform the act, and so forth. When several different strands of evidence are taken together and complement each other, then and only then can a strong case be made for reaching a conclusion.

The same holds true for looking at the different behavior patterns associated with each of the seven aspects. A single disturbed behavior pattern for characteristic #7, Physical, associated with a majority of normal adaptability patterns, would not necessarily indicate a pattern of emotional disturbance or a major emotional problem. But disturbed behavior patterns for all seven characteristics would be very strong indicators that mental imbalance is present and accountable and needs to be addressed.

WHAT'S IN A NAME?

Although the names of the seven characteristics are common words, please do not assume that you understand exactly what they mean. These are everyday words, but they are being used with greater precision in order to carefully distinguish and categorize these behaviors. Therefore, they take on a more specific meaning in the context of the test of adaptability. The terms are not meant to contradict everyday use, but are being used in a more particular way. *Please do not assume that you know the intended meaning. Read the following definitions and examples.*

Characteristic #1: Tension

Tension refers to the level and impact of anxiety in yourself. Signs of tension include agitation, fingernail-biting, sweating, rapid breathing, and a sense of physical tightness. The famous tension-headache commercials might be examples of the characteristic of tension as used in this book, but most cases include other dimensions, such as irritability and physical manifestations of tension that are properly categorized as relating to characteristics #2, Mood, and #7, Physical.

A certain amount of anxiety or tension in everyday life is both unavoidable and necessary. Not to feel nervous or tense at all on a first date, when attending an important business conference, or upon delivering a school address is uncommon and not necessarily desirable. In fact, tension plays a vital role in many tasks, contributing to and improving performance. A common example is the tension and excitement an athlete or musician may feel just before the start of an athletic contest or a performance. These cases, depending on degree and intensity, would be normal instances of healthy or positive tension. What would be abnormal would be such an intense degree of tension that an individual could not perform at all, as in the case of a performer's stage fright or of a young business executive's getting so keyed up before a conference that he is unable to effectively present his thoughts and suggestions in a coherent manner.

The cause of tension is an integral component in evaluating the positive and negative aspects of tension as a measure of adaptability. Accordingly, aspect #1, Tension, will also be used to refer to the cause of tension in the presentation of the five stages of adaptability.

Characteristic #2: Mood

Mood refers to how a person feels. Everyone experiences different moods at different times. There are moods of happiness, sadness, optimism, pessimism, or just feeling numb. There are irritable moods and pleasant moods. Even a grumpy, irritable boss who never seems to be pleasant may have moods of lesser irritability. As such, a mood is a relative term that depends in large part on your general personality type. What is an optimistic mood for a cynic may resemble a pessimistic mood for a wide-eyed idealist.

In evaluating mood, it is best to judge by your own experience of emotions, and not by stereotyped images of joy or sadness presented in films and television.

Nevertheless, there are objective criteria for evaluating changes in mood and the influence of mood upon your character as a measure of mental health. Moods usually have a direct cause and are of short or moderate duration. Failing an examination, not getting an expected raise at work, losing a baseball game after making a crucial error— these are the kinds of events that provoke moods of sadness, irritability, or depression, depending on individual variations. This is normal and to be expected, and quite intense moods might result. It would be considered abnormal if such events created a depressed mood that lasted days, or even weeks, and was not in accordance with more positive experiences that took place after the initial disappointment. In cases of severe mental disorder, a mood of depression or numbness may so overwhelm an individual that he or she is incapable of responding to his or her environment at all.

A good guide toward evaluating your pattern and experience of moods is to look at your sense of humor. A person who is not suffering from mental problems does not lose his or her sense of humor for long, even in the midst of intense feelings of anger, frustration, or sadness. This person is able to step back and laugh at himself or herself and not take life so seriously. Someone with a good sense of humor is also able to appreciate the feelings of others and to allow them, through jokes and other affectionately intended overtures, to draw him or her out of sadness or anger.

Loss of sense of humor or the formation of an intense pattern of humor might include a display of a permanent hostile wit that manifests itself through biting sarcasm, both in reference to others and oneself. This would be an indication that, in terms of mood experiences, an individual is suffering from some form of mental stress. Total loss of sense of humor or the inability to take anything lightly or playfully is associated with more severe mental disorders.

Characteristic #3: Thought

The behavior category of Thought refers to what a person thinks about. Thought behavior is classified in different ways, including appropriate versus inappropriate, continuous versus periodic, and mature versus regressive.

An example of inappropriate thought would be for a student taking an examination to be unable to stop thinking about his or her upcoming vacation throughout the entire examination. Periodic thoughts are those that recur at intervals but are interrupted by other thoughts. Continuous thinking is the ability to start a line of reasoning and to bring it to a conclusion without other thoughts interfering. Regressive thoughts refer mostly to fantasies about past situations that are not in touch with present circumstances. Mature thoughts are ones that take account of yourself and the world as it is and relate them to positive action.

A danger signal pointing to a breakdown in thought behavior is apparent when thoughts are no longer related to concrete events and do not lead to action. A common initial phase of such a breakdown is circular worrying (or rumination). A certain amount of this is probably inevitable and in its mildest form includes double- or triple-checking shopping lists or the car before making a trip. But more severe circular worrying is obvious when someone thinks about all the things that could possibly go wrong without being able to relate the worry to any form of constructive action. An example would be someone worrying about an upcoming job interview in this way: "The interviewer won't like me. He probably saw me fumble the ball in the big game last year. The sun will shine in my eyes and I'll have to squint and look stupid. He'll get a phone call during the interview and I won't know what to do. I'll start to sweat. He probably knows that my brother was just fired. If he saw the game last year I'm finished for sure. He probably doesn't like Catholics." This type of worry is also known as "negative self-talk."

Such circular worrying before a stressful event (such as a job interview), though unproductive, is not necessarily particularly abnormal. Worrying in this fashion about many, or most, events in your life would be abnormal. This kind of thinking leads to the inability to make decisions, which is a sign of more severe emotional problems. In extreme cases, obsessive thoughts and gross perceptual distortions totally isolate a person's thinking from the everyday world and are sure signs that the individual is under intensive mental stress.

A word of caution in evaluating thought behavior: Most people at some time in their life experience all the different forms of thought behavior. *The key to evaluating your level of thought behavior is to focus on your most common daily and weekly patterns, not the occasional exceptions.*

Characteristic #4: Activity

Activity refers to what a person is interested in and does. Activity includes work, play, hobbies, and any task or project that engages both mind and body. The kind and nature of activity in which you engage is related to your energy level. When your energy level is low you are less likely to engage in new activities and more likely to feel fatigue or exhaustion, rather than enthusiasm or satisfied expended energy at the end of an activity.

The activity of a healthy person is characterized by an interest in different kinds of activities and a sense of competence in many areas of both personal and group activities. *The ability to take risks, to be mediocre in some areas, and to try again after failing is characteristic of a healthy pattern of activities.* Under normal circumstances, an individual is able to engage both in continuous activities, such as working on an assembly line for several hours without stopping, and in uneven activities, such as preparing a meal in which he or she might be called upon to add spices to a stew at different intervals and change temperatures, while playing a game of bridge with friends.

When activity becomes compulsive or ritualistic—that is, you exercise only because it is good for you, or play cards because you promised the guys but are detached from the activity and not really a part of it—then something is wrong. Notions such as just going through the motions or feeling only relief and no satisfaction when the day's activities are over ("Well, I got through another day") are signs of mental stress.

Some key areas to focus on in evaluating your activity behavior is the rhythm of your life: *Are you often hyperactive without really accomplishing anything? Do you do only things that are "important," never taking time off to play or rest or do something silly or inconsequential? Do you follow a rigid set of activities with infrequent changes?*

Characteristic #5: Organization/Control

Organization/Control is essentially the quality of self-discipline. It refers to your capacity and freedom to plan and carry out whatever you wish to do. Organization/Control behavior affects both work and play and manifests itself in a variety of ways.

The most common indicators are the ways in which you organize the major activities of your life. Do you take on and finish tasks on schedule without difficulty? Or do you overextend your abilities in an attempt to do more than you comfortably can in the time at your disposal? Do you need constant encouragement from others to keep at a difficult or tedious job, or are you able to set your own pace and provide your own motivation and self-discipline? Do you need a perfect work environment, or are you able to handle ambiguity and disturbances without becoming unsettled? Do you learn from experience or act impulsively, not really examining the pros and cons of different problem-solving strategies?

In evaluating your Organization/Control behavior, a key measure is to see how you handle unexpected and unpredictable events. It is normal to experience some anxiety and frustration

when things don't turn out as expected—a parade prevents
you from going home from work the usual way, someone
gets sick and you are forced to take on greater responsibility
at home or at work, you plan an outdoor barbecue and it
rains, and so forth. Do you go into a rage, cursing the parade, fellow occupants in the car, and your spouse when you
get home? Or do you just curse the parade and your bad
luck without yelling at everyone in sight? When it rains at
the barbecue, are you able to set up an alternative plan in
the house and maintain the pleasant spirit of the party? Or
do you get depressed and wish your guests would go home
and leave you alone to suffer your rotten luck? The examples here are minor cases but are indicators of the kinds of
situations that enable you to judge your level of self-control
and your ability to control your internal feelings. It's easy to
be a considerate and loving person when you feel like a million dollars, but *it's how you behave when you feel disappointed
that often indicates your Organization/Control behavior.*

Characteristic #6: Interpersonal Relationships

*The aspect of Interpersonal Relationships refers to the style and sta-
bility of your relations with parents, colleagues, co-workers, neighbors, friends, and others. Are your relations intimate or superficial?
Do you have a range of different kinds of relationships? Can you be
a friend as well as have friends?* Do you always insist on getting
your own way? Are you overly anxious about pleasing others? Or are you able to have a real interchange with others
in which you experience a variety of roles and feelings at
different times as circumstances vary?

Some key areas to watch in terms of interpersonal behavior include whether or not you bear grudges and whether you pattern your relationships along strict lines of emotional dependence or manipulation. Any overly rigid pattern
is an indication that you are responding with only part of
your personality toward others. If you mold all your relationships along predetermined lines, it is an indication that you
are not really responding to others but are reacting to inner

conflicts in ways that may have been appropriate in the past or with a specific relative or close friend. *Each person is different, and your relationships with people should realistically reflect these differences.* In other words, if all your relationships with others are of the same general type, you are both giving and calling upon only a limited aspect of your own personality and the personalities of others.

If your relationships with others are generally characterized by destructive patterns, with grudges rising out of misunderstandings of a repetitive nature, you could probably use some help. *A good indicator to keep an eye on in this respect is the relative stability of your relationships. Are you engaged in long-term, stable relationships, or is your life characterized by short-term, up-and-down relationships of an ambiguous variety?*

Characteristic #7: Physical

Physical behavior is perhaps that most overlooked by people in assessing their mental health. Research has demonstrated that many mental diseases are closely linked to physical symptoms. Stress has been shown to alter the production of hormones and chemicals in the body, leading to a variety of symptoms.

In this book, physical behavior refers not only to how well a person feels but also to the presence or absence of bodily symptoms. Common areas in which mental problems may manifest themselves include changes in eating and sleeping patterns, gastrointestinal disorders, skin blemishes, headaches, insomnia, and drug and alcohol abuse or addiction.

Many of these disorders may have causes unrelated to mental stress, but their existence will contribute to heightening existing mental problems and provoking new difficulties. Of course, there are many cases of gastrointestinal problems (gas, heartburn, constipation, diarrhea, etc.) and headaches that are temporary problems created by stress or by eating too much or the wrong foods. However, these same symptoms, if they recur over a long period of time, are indicators of mental or possibly physical ailments as well.

One further note: When we say that a physical symp-

tom, such as a pain in the chest or the back, is a manifestation of a mental problem or of mental stress, this does not
imply that the physical pain is not real and disturbing; nor
does it imply that the physical pain itself should not be
treated.

3
····

The First Test of Adaptability

GETTING READY FOR TEST #1

In truth, we might prefer that you first read and understand the Theory of the Five Stages of Emotional Well-Being *before* you take the test. We know, however, that most people don't like to read through theory. After all, you bought the book because you want to take the test! Some of you wish to take the plunge now. Go ahead, jump right in. Remember, you can always read the theory *after* you take your first test. In fact, we strongly urge you to take the second test (Test #2, on page 107) at a future date to increase the reliability of your test scores.

Some of you are more methodical or cautious by nature and may wish to read the theory *first,* then take the first test. This is an equally valid and intelligent way to approach these self-tests. You be the judge. Decide which way feels best to you and have a go at it.

Remember, it's supposed to be fun!

HOW TO USE THE CHECKLISTS

Now, whether or not you fully understand the theory and the nature of the symptoms, you are ready to use the Emotional Well-Being Checklist.

• The checklist consists of seven subtests, corresponding to each of the seven aspects of human behavior. Each checklist contains all the possible behavior patterns and symptoms that correspond to each of the five stages of mental health. Your job is simply to check off those behavior patterns and symptoms that most accurately and honestly describe your feelings and actions for each of the seven characteristics of behavior.

• This checking-off will give you a mini-picture of your state of mental health for each of the seven characteristics. Then, with the aid of the point score system, you can calculate a total score for each subarea, which will be used to diagnose your overall emotional well-being.

• Examples are provided after each checklist for the calculation of your point scores. We've also given you four examples of mental health bar graphs with full explanations.

Two important reminders:

1. It is expected that your behavior for each of the seven characteristics will include symptoms from different stages of mental health. Do not be alarmed if your behavior includes symptoms from each of the five stages, from normal to disturbed behavior. Given the complex and varied nature of human emotional well-being, this is quite possible. The charts are devised so that these apparent contradictions will be dealt with through the use of point scores in the calculation of your overall mental health bar graph.

2. If you do not understand a symptom or typical behavior pattern, do not guess or leave it blank. After each symptom, in parentheses, is listed the page number on which the symptom can be found and explained. Go forward in the text to the page where each symptom is presented in the appropriate stage of mental health to which it corresponds. Read down until you come to the symptom in question and the full explanation that accompanies it. *All terms used in the checklists are fully explained in Appendix A and have been carefully organized to facilitate easy recognition.* Such cross-checking is essential if you are to avoid guessing and you wish to achieve an accurate assessment of your own emotional well-being.

CHECKLIST OF YOUR EMOTIONAL WELL-BEING

Characteristic #1: Tension

Do you have these typical behaviors and symptoms?

____ 1. Your tension has a cause in the present or past. (p. 142)

____ 2. You can do something that helps you to relieve your tension. (p. 142)

____ 3. You have clear-cut signs of tension (agitation, rapid breathing, sweating). (p. 152)

____ 4. Your tension may sometimes inhibit your ability to work. (p. 152)

____ 5. You have signs of tension with no apparent cause. (p. 159)

____ 6. Your tension inhibits your work most of the time. (p. 159)

____ 7. You are often dependent on strong defenses to make your tension bearable. (p. 175)

____ 8. You have periods of nearly unbearable anxiety with no obvious cause or understanding. (p. 175)

____ 9. Your tension feels unbearable without medication. (p. 186)

____ 10. Your tension is only relieved by disturbed thinking (distortions, hallucinations, grossly inappropriate plans). (p. 186)

Characteristic #2: Mood

Do you have these typical behaviors and symptoms?

____ 1. Your mood swings have a specific cause. (p. 143)

____ 2. You usually have a sense of humor. (p. 143)

____ 3. Your moods can be intense, but they pass within a short time. (p. 143)

____ 4. You are often easily upset, or you are often moody, or intolerant of others. (p. 153)

____ 5. You use explosive humor as a tension release. (p. 153)

____ 6. Your moods often last for long periods. (p. 160)

____ 7. You have periodic hysterical behavior. (p. 160)

____ 8. You have strong emotional expressions, often without apparent reason. (p. 160)

____ 9. You often use a hostile sense of humor (sarcasm, etc.). (p. 160)

____ 10. You have mild ongoing fears and phobias. (p. 160)

____ 11. You take unnecessary risks to overcome your fears. (p. 160)

____ 12. You have specific blocked or flattened emotions (e.g. love, hate). (p. 160)

____ 13. Your background moods often affect your ability to work, love, and play. (p. 176)

____ 14. You often have ongoing depressed, unhappy states. (p. 176)

____ 15. You have made suicide attempts, or you have frequent thoughts about suicide. (p. 176)

____ 16. You can get "high" on ideas, but you have problems in following through. (p. 176)

____ 17. You have self-destructive, risk-taking behavior. (p. 176)

____ 18. You often have periods of hysterical behavior (tantrums, emotional outbursts, or destructive behavior). (p. 176)

____ 19. You experience delusions, thought disorders, or hallucinations. (pp. 187–188)

___ 20. You have severe depressions, are often unreachable, or you shut down your work or love involvements. (p. 188)

Characteristic #3: Thought

Do you have these typical behaviors and symptoms?

___ 1. You are able to gather and process information easily. (p. 144)

___ 2. Your thoughts, of whatever kind, do not upset you for long. (p. 144)

___ 3. Your thoughts usually help you to carry out your plans. (p. 144)

___ 4. Your thoughts are intensely, narrowly focused on your task or problem. (p. 153)

___ 5. You experience tension release through your thoughts (e.g., passive, aggressive, or sexual thoughts). (p. 153)

___ 6. You often block out all but important information. (p. 153)

___ 7. You have a tendency to analyze rather than experience your feelings. (p. 163)

___ 8. You often question your ability to feel important emotions. (p. 163)

___ 9. You often experience obsessive worrying or negative self-talk. (p. 163)

___ 10. You often have chronic distortions of reality. (p. 178)

___ 11. You are often alert to an unspecified danger. (p. 178)

___ 12. You often screen out or miss important information. (p. 178)

___ 13. You have repetitive or bothersome thoughts that disrupt your living. (p. 178)

___ 14. Your thoughts often stop you from experiencing strong feelings (e.g., love, anger). (p. 178)

___ 15. You have great difficulty in making decisions. (p. 178)

___ 16. You have continual obsessive thoughts. (p. 190)

___ 17. You have gross perceptual distortions (i.e., visual or auditory hallucinations). (p. 190)

Characteristic #4: Activity

Do you have these typical behaviors and symptoms?

___ 1. You have enthusiasm and interest in doing and participating, and you have a sense of competence. (p. 145)

___ 2. You can take risks and be resilient; you can dare to be mediocre, or even fail and try again. (p. 145)

___ 3. You can handle either continuous ongoing activity or stop-and-start types of activity. (p. 145)

___ 4. According to your temperament, you usually have lots of activity or little activity. (p. 154)

___ 5. You often have anxiety about new risks, or you often feel overloaded. (p. 155)

___ 6. You often use ritualistic words and behavior. (p. 155)

___ 7. You are often hyperactive with no particular purpose or result. (p. 164)

___ 8. You require much inspiration or feedback in order to work adequately. (p. 164)

___ 9. You are usually unable to take risks. (p. 164)

___ 10. You generally avoid new activities. (p. 180)

___ 11. Your coping activities (skills) are no longer able to relieve your tension. (p. 180)

___ 12. You have no pleasure in your accomplishments, your activities are often solitary, and you feel pain if they are not completed. (p. 180)

___ 13. You are frequently engaged in compulsive, ritualistic activities. (p. 191)

___ 14. You have extreme difficulty in changing your patterns of activity. (p. 191)

Characteristic #5: Organization/Control

Do you have these typical behaviors and symptoms?

___ 1. You are able to sit still and address yourself to tasks for the necessary periods of time. (p. 147)

___ 2. You can work in the absence of inspiration or feedback. (p. 147)

___ 3. You can plan and carry out solutions to multi-step problems. (p. 147)

___ 4. You are able to learn from your own experience. (p. 147)

___ 5. You are free to act differently under varying circumstances. (p. 147)

___ 6. Your anxiety often stimulates you to take action. (p. 155)

___ 7. You often find yourself lying or cheating when you are under pressure. (p. 155)

___ 8. You are becoming increasingly rigid: you require clearcut guidelines, or you need perfect conditions in order to function. (p. 166)

___ 9. You regularly feel that you are being overextended. (p. 166)

___ 10. Unpredictable events are often able to disrupt or to negatively influence your performance. (p. 166)

___ 11. You are involved in occasional impulsive behaviors. (p. 166)

___ 12. Your personal rituals often interfere with your work (e.g. sharpening pencils). (p. 166)

___ 13. You have a limited capacity for self-insight and for change. (p. 166)

___ 14. Your behavior is often mechanical. (p. 181)

___ 15. Unexpected minor events often cause you to stop work or to stop activities of love and play. (p. 181)

___ 16. In order to function, you often find yourself performing obsessive rituals. (p. 181)

___ 17. You often display impulsive behavior that disrupts your plans; you don't learn from your mistakes or experience. (p. 181)

___ 18. You have very little self-control; you are easily influenced by outside suggestion or by inner feelings. (p. 192)

___ 19. Your feelings generally make it impossible to work. (p. 192)

___ 20. You are often involved in disturbing, impulsive behavior. (p. 192)

Characteristic #6:
Interpersonal Relationships

Do you have these typical behaviors and symptoms?

___ 1. You can be a friend and you can have friends. (p. 148)

___ 2. You have an increasing capacity for intimacy with others. (p. 148)

___ 3. When you withdraw emotionally or become aggressive, it usually has a clear cause, and it soon passes. (p. 148)

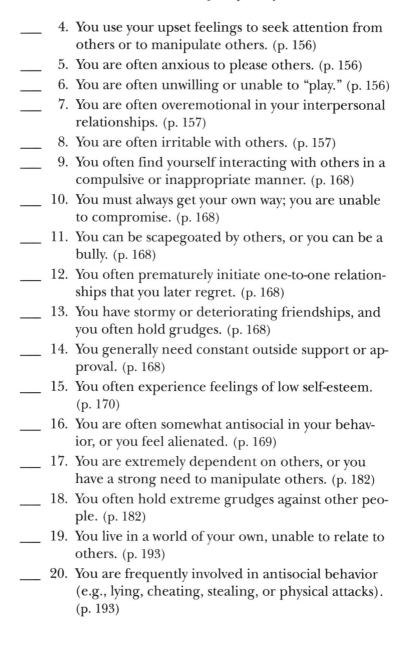

___ 4. You use your upset feelings to seek attention from others or to manipulate others. (p. 156)

___ 5. You are often anxious to please others. (p. 156)

___ 6. You are often unwilling or unable to "play." (p. 156)

___ 7. You are often overemotional in your interpersonal relationships. (p. 157)

___ 8. You are often irritable with others. (p. 157)

___ 9. You often find yourself interacting with others in a compulsive or inappropriate manner. (p. 168)

___ 10. You must always get your own way; you are unable to compromise. (p. 168)

___ 11. You can be scapegoated by others, or you can be a bully. (p. 168)

___ 12. You often prematurely initiate one-to-one relationships that you later regret. (p. 168)

___ 13. You have stormy or deteriorating friendships, and you often hold grudges. (p. 168)

___ 14. You generally need constant outside support or approval. (p. 168)

___ 15. You often experience feelings of low self-esteem. (p. 170)

___ 16. You are often somewhat antisocial in your behavior, or you feel alienated. (p. 169)

___ 17. You are extremely dependent on others, or you have a strong need to manipulate others. (p. 182)

___ 18. You often hold extreme grudges against other people. (p. 182)

___ 19. You live in a world of your own, unable to relate to others. (p. 193)

___ 20. You are frequently involved in antisocial behavior (e.g., lying, cheating, stealing, or physical attacks). (p. 193)

Characteristic #7: Physical

Do you have these typical behaviors and symptoms?

____ 1. You have stable patterns of eating, good digestion, healthy skin, and normal breathing, sleeping, and weight. (p. 150)

____ 2. You have relatively quick recovery from an illness or an accident. (p. 150)

____ 3. You have a sense of physical well-being. (p. 150)

____ 4. You have many fluctuations in eating and sleeping patterns, or changes in weight, minor gastrointestinal (GI) problems, blemishes. (p. 158)

____ 5. You often feel tense, tired, or exhausted. (p. 158)

____ 6. You intentionally find yourself using drugs or alcohol in order to cope. (p. 158)

____ 7. You have periodic skin blemishes, GI problems, obesity, lack of appetite, sleep disturbances, or headaches. (p. 171)

____ 8. You have physical tics and/or stuttering. (p. 171)

____ 9. You have many complaints about your health, often with no clearly defined symptoms. (p. 172)

____ 10. You often use drugs and alcohol or seek medical help to "feel better." (p. 171)

____ 11. You are involved in episodes of drug abuse, often reinforced by your friends or contacts. (p. 171)

____ 12. You appear stiff and/or uptight in your physical mannerisms. (p. 183)

____ 13. You have ongoing psychosomatic problems—ulcers, colitis, insomnia, migraines, absence of menses, anorexia—often without a clear-cut cause. (p. 183)

____ 14. You medicate yourself with drugs or alcohol, often alone, in order to cope. (p. 183)

____ 15. You are continally exhausted, without apparent reason. (p. 183)

___ 16. You display bizarre physical postures. (p. 194)

___ 17. You have many ongoing physical problems, some without apparent cause. (p. 194)

___ 18. You have serious addictions (e.g., drugs and alcohol, sexual behavior, eating disorders, gambling). (p. 195)

Checklist for Characteristic #1: Tension

Refer to the checklists on the preceding pages. Transfer your checks to the boxes on this page by shading the boxes that correspond to your Tension behavior.

Remember, your behavior may fall into several stages of emotional well-being.

NORMAL	STATE OF ALERT	ANXIOUS COPING	ANXIOUS CHARACTER	DISTURBED BEHAVIOR
1. ☐				
2. ☐				
	3. ☐			
	4. ☐			
		5. ☐		
		6. ☐		
			7. ☐	
			8. ☐	
				9. ☐
				10. ☐

To Calculate Point Score for Tension Behavior

1. Fill in the number of points for each symptom you checked off in the Tension diagnostic chart on the preceding page.

2. Add up your score for this characteristic, writing the total in the space provided.

3. Now add the number of symptoms you checked off (this will be a number between 1 and 10) and write this number beneath your total score.

4. Divide the total score by the number of symptoms reported. The result is your score for mental adaptability as measured by Tension behavior.

5. Record this number in the appropriate box and refer to it when you have completed your self-diagnosis and are ready to calculate your overall mental health adaptability score with the aid of the mental health bar graph.

SYMPTOM	POINTS	YOUR SCORE	WORK SPACE
1	10	_____	
2	10	_____	
3	20	_____	
4	20	_____	
5	30	_____	
6	30	_____	
7	40	_____	
8	40	_____	
9	50	_____	
10	50	_____	

Total score _____ divided by number of symptoms
recorded _____ equals Tension point score. [_____]

Example: If you checked Tension symptoms 1, 2, 3, 6, and 9, you would proceed thus:

1	10
2	10
3	20
6	30
9	50

120 = Total score

   5   Number of symptoms

A total score of 120 divided by 5 symptoms equals a Tension point score of 24.

You have just finished the first of seven mini-charts. The procedure for the next six is the same. *Be sure you understand each symptom before using these checklists.*

Checklist for Characteristic #2: Mood

Shade in the boxes that correspond to your Mood behavior.
   Remember, your behavior may fall into several stages of emotional well-being.

NORMAL	STATE OF ALERT	ANXIOUS COPING	ANXIOUS CHARACTER	DISTURBED BEHAVIOR
1. ☐				
2. ☐				
3. ☐				
	4. ☐			
	5. ☐			
		6. ☐		
		7. ☐		
		8. ☐		
		9. ☐		
		10. ☐		
		11. ☐		
		12. ☐		
			13. ☐	
			14. ☐	
			15. ☐	
			16. ☐	
			17. ☐	
			18. ☐	
				19. ☐
				20. ☐

To Calculate Point Score for Mood Behavior

1. Fill in the number of points for each symptom you checked off in the Mood diagnostic chart on the preceding page.

2. Add up your score for this characteristic, writing the total in the space provided.

3. Now add the number of symptoms you checked off (this will be a number between 1 and 20) and write this number beneath your total score.

4. Divide the total score by the number of symptoms reported. The result is your score for mental adaptability as measured by Mood behavior.

5. Record this number in the appropriate box and refer to it when you have completed your self-diagnosis and are ready to calculate your overall mental health adaptability score with the aid of the mental health bar graph.

SYMPTOM	POINTS	YOUR SCORE	WORK SPACE
1	10	_____	
2	10	_____	
3	10	_____	
4	20	_____	
5	20	_____	
6	30	_____	
7	30	_____	
8	30	_____	
9	30	_____	
10	30	_____	
11	30	_____	
12	30	_____	
13	40	_____	
14	40	_____	
15	40	_____	
16	40	_____	
17	40	_____	

SYMPTOM	POINTS	YOUR SCORE	WORK SPACE
18	40	_____	
19	50	_____	
20	50	_____	

Total score _____ divided by number of symptoms
recorded _____ equals Mood point score.   [_____]

Example: If you checked Mood symptoms 1, 2, 3, 4, 5,
6, 7, 10, 13, 14, and 16, you would proceed thus:

1	10
2	10
3	10
4	20
5	20
6	30
7	30
10	30
13	40
14	40
16	40

280 = Total score
11   Number of symptoms

A total score of 280 divided by 11 symptoms equals a Mood
point score of 25.5.

Checklist for Characteristic #3: Thought

Shade in the boxes that correspond to your Thought behavior.
Remember, your behavior may fall into several stages of emotional well-being.

NORMAL	STATE OF ALERT	ANXIOUS COPING	ANXIOUS CHARACTER	DISTURBED BEHAVIOR
1. ☐				
2. ☐				
3. ☐				
	4. ☐			
	5. ☐			
	6. ☐			
		7. ☐		
		8. ☐		
		9. ☐		
			10. ☐	
			11. ☐	
			12. ☐	
			13. ☐	
			14. ☐	
			15. ☐	
				16. ☐
				17. ☐

To Calculate Point Score for Thought Behavior

1. Fill in the number of points for each symptom you checked off in the Thought diagnostic chart on the preceding page.
2. Add up your score for this characteristic, writing the total in the space provided.
3. Now add the number of symptoms you checked off (this will be a number between 1 and 17) and write this number beneath your total score.
4. Divide the total score by the number of symptoms reported. The result is your score for mental adaptability as measured by Thought behavior.
5. Record this number in the appropriate box and refer to it when you have completed your self-diagnosis and are ready to calculate your overall mental health adaptability score with the aid of the mental health bar graph.

SYMPTOM	POINTS	YOUR SCORE	WORK SPACE
1	10	_____	
2	10	_____	
3	10	_____	
4	20	_____	
5	20	_____	
6	20	_____	
7	30	_____	
8	30	_____	
9	30	_____	
10	40	_____	
11	40	_____	
12	40	_____	
13	40	_____	
14	40	_____	
15	40	_____	
16	50	_____	
17	50	_____	

Total score _____ divided by number of symptoms
recorded _____ equals Thought point score. [   ]

Example: If you checked Thought symptoms 1, 2, 3, 4,
6, 9, 13, and 15, you would proceed thus:

1	10
2	10
3	10
4	20
6	20
9	30
13	40
15	40

    180 = Total score
      8   Number of symptoms

A total score of 180 divided by 8 symptoms equals a
Thought point score of 22.5.

Checklist for Characteristic #4: Activity

Shade in the boxes that correspond to your Activity behavior.
   Remember, your behavior may fall into several stages of emotional well-being.

NORMAL	STATE OF ALERT	ANXIOUS COPING	ANXIOUS CHARACTER	DISTURBED BEHAVIOR
1. ☐				
2. ☐				
3. ☐				
	4. ☐			
	5. ☐			
	6. ☐			
		7. ☐		
		8. ☐		
		9. ☐		
			10. ☐	
			11. ☐	
			12. ☐	
				13. ☐
				14. ☐

To Calculate Point Score for Activity Behavior

1. Fill in the number of points for each symptom you checked off in the Activity diagnostic chart on the preceding page.
2. Add up your score for this characteristic, writing the total in the space provided.
3. Now add the number of symptoms you checked off (this will be a number between 1 and 14) and write this number beneath your total score.
4. Divide the total score by the number of symptoms reported. The result is your score for mental adaptability as measured by Activity behavior.
5. Record this number in the appropriate box and refer to it when you have completed your self-diagnosis and are ready to calculate your overall mental health adaptability score with the aid of the mental health bar graph.

SYMPTOM	POINTS	YOUR SCORE	WORK SPACE
1	10	_____	
2	10	_____	
3	10	_____	
4	20	_____	
5	20	_____	
6	20	_____	
7	30	_____	
8	30	_____	
9	30	_____	
10	40	_____	
11	40	_____	
12	40	_____	
13	50	_____	
14	50	_____	

Total score _____ divided by number of symptoms
recorded _____ equals Activity point score. [_____]

Example: If you checked Activity symptoms 1, 2, 3, 4, 8, and 10, you would proceed thus:

1	10
2	10
3	10
4	20
8	30
10	40

<u>120</u> = Total score
6   Number of symptoms

A total score of 120 divided by 6 symptoms equals an Activity point score of 20.

Checklist for Characteristic #5:
Organization/Control

Shade in the boxes that correspond to your Organization/Control behavior.

   Remember, your behavior may fall into several stages of emotional well-being.

NORMAL	STATE OF ALERT	ANXIOUS COPING	ANXIOUS CHARACTER	DISTURBED BEHAVIOR
1. ☐				
2. ☐				
3. ☐				
4. ☐				
5. ☐				
	6. ☐			
	7. ☐			
		8. ☐		
		9. ☐		
		10. ☐		
		11. ☐		
		12. ☐		
		13. ☐		
			14. ☐	
			15. ☐	
			16. ☐	
			17. ☐	
				18. ☐
				19. ☐
				20. ☐

To Calculate Point Score for Organization/Control Behavior

1. Fill in the number of points for each symptom you checked off in the Organization/Control diagnostic chart on the preceding page.
2. Add up your score for this characteristic, writing the total in the space provided.
3. Now add the number of symptoms you checked off (this will be a number between 1 and 20) and write this number beneath your total score.
4. Divide the total score by the number of symptoms reported. The result is your score for mental adaptability as measured by Organization/Control behavior.
5. Record this number in the appropriate box and refer to it when you have completed your self-diagnosis and are ready to calculate your overall mental health adaptability score with the aid of the mental health bar graph.

SYMPTOM	POINTS	YOUR SCORE	WORK SPACE
1	10	_____	
2	10	_____	
3	10	_____	
4	10	_____	
5	10	_____	
6	20	_____	
7	20	_____	
8	30	_____	
9	30	_____	
10	30	_____	
11	30	_____	
12	30	_____	
13	30	_____	
14	40	_____	
15	40	_____	
16	40	_____	

SYMPTOM	POINTS	YOUR SCORE	WORK SPACE
17	40	_____	
18	50	_____	
19	50	_____	
20	50	_____	

Total score _____ divided by number of symptoms recorded _____ equals Organization/Control point score. [_____]

Example: If you checked Organization/Control symptoms 3, 4, 5, 7, 8, 10, 11, and 18, you would proceed thus:

3	10
4	10
5	10
7	20
8	30
10	30
11	30
18	50

$\overline{190}$ = Total score

8 Number of symptoms

A total score of 190 divided by 8 symptoms equals an Organization/Control point score of 23.75.

Checklist for Characteristic #6:
Interpersonal Relationships

Shade in the boxes that correspond to your Interpersonal Relationships behavior.

Remember, your behavior may fall into several stages of emotional well-being.

NORMAL	STATE OF ALERT	ANXIOUS COPING	ANXIOUS CHARACTER	DISTURBED BEHAVIOR
1. ☐				
2. ☐				
3. ☐				
	4. ☐			
	5. ☐			
	6. ☐			
	7. ☐			
	8. ☐			
		9. ☐		
		10. ☐		
		11. ☐		
		12. ☐		
		13. ☐		
		14. ☐		
		15. ☐		
		16. ☐		
			17. ☐	
			18. ☐	
				19. ☐
				20. ☐

To Calculate Point Score for Interpersonal Relationships Behavior

1. Fill in the number of points for each symptom you checked off in the Interpersonal Relationships diagnostic chart on the preceding page.
2. Add up your score for this characteristic, writing the total in the space provided.
3. Now add the number of symptoms you checked off (this will be a number between 1 and 20) and write this number beneath your total score.
4. Divide the total score by the number of symptoms reported. The result is your score for mental adaptability as measured by Interpersonal Relationships behavior.
5. Record this number in the appropriate box and refer to it when you have completed your self-diagnosis and are ready to calculate your overall mental health adaptability score with the aid of the mental health bar graph.

SYMPTOM	POINTS	YOUR SCORE	WORK SPACE
1	10	_____	
2	10	_____	
3	10	_____	
4	20	_____	
5	20	_____	
6	20	_____	
7	20	_____	
8	20	_____	
9	30	_____	
10	30	_____	
11	30	_____	
12	30	_____	
13	30	_____	
14	30	_____	
15	30	_____	
16	30	_____	

SYMPTOM	POINTS	YOUR SCORE	WORK SPACE
17	40	_____	
18	40	_____	
19	50	_____	
20	50	_____	

Total score _____ divided by number of symptoms recorded _____ equals Interpersonal Relationships point score. [_____]

Example: If you checked Interpersonal Relationships symptoms 1, 2, 3, 5, 7, 15, and 18, you would proceed thus:

1	10
2	10
3	10
5	20
7	20
15	30
18	40

$\overline{140}$ = Total score

7   Number of symptoms

A total score of 140 divided by 7 symptoms equals an Interpersonal Relationships point score of 20.

Checklist for Characteristic #7: Physical

Shade in the boxes that correspond to your Physical behavior.
   Remember, your behavior may fall into several stages of emotional well-being.

NORMAL	STATE OF ALERT	ANXIOUS COPING	ANXIOUS CHARACTER	DISTURBED BEHAVIOR
1. ☐				
2. ☐				
3. ☐				
	4. ☐			
	5. ☐			
	6. ☐			
		7. ☐		
		8. ☐		
		9. ☐		
		10. ☐		
		11. ☐		
			12. ☐	
			13. ☐	
			14. ☐	
			15. ☐	
				16. ☐
				17. ☐
				18. ☐

To Calculate Point Score for Physical Behavior

1. Fill in the number of points for each symptom you checked off in the Physical diagnostic chart on the preceding page.
2. Add up your score for this characteristic, writing the total in the space provided.
3. Now add the number of symptoms you checked off (this will be a number between 1 and 18) and write this number beneath your total score.
4. Divide the total score by the number of symptoms reported. The result is your score for mental adaptability as measured by Physical behavior.
5. Record this number in the appropriate box and refer to it when you have completed your self-diagnosis and are ready to calculate your overall mental health adaptability score with the aid of the mental health bar graph.

SYMPTOM	POINTS	YOUR SCORE	WORK SPACE
1	10	_____	
2	10	_____	
3	10	_____	
4	20	_____	
5	20	_____	
6	20	_____	
7	30	_____	
8	30	_____	
9	30	_____	
10	30	_____	
11	30	_____	
12	40	_____	
13	40	_____	
14	40	_____	
15	40	_____	
16	50	_____	
17	50	_____	
18	50	_____	

Total score _____ divided by number of symptoms
recorded _____ equals Physical point score. [   ]

    Example: If you checked Physical symptoms 1, 2, 4, and
5, you would proceed thus:

1	10
2	10
4	20
5	50

     60 = Total score
      4   Number of symptoms

A total score of 60 divided by 4 symptoms equals a Physical
point score of 15.

YOUR EMOTIONAL WELL-BEING
BAR GRAPH

Now that you have computed your total scores for each of
the seven aspects, you will be able to fill in the bar graph
with a picture of your mental health.

    Simply shade in the area for each characteristic that lies
to the left of your point score. The result is a visual image of
your present state of emotional well-being. Four examples,
complete with bar graphs, are provided in Chapter 4, Test
Interpretation and Evaluation.

Mental Health Bar Graph

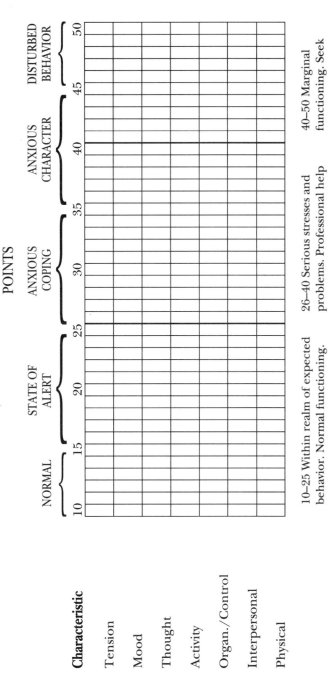

POINTS

Characteristic	NORMAL		STATE OF ALERT		ANXIOUS COPING		ANXIOUS CHARACTER		DISTURBED BEHAVIOR	
	10	15	20	25	30	35	40	45	50	
Tension										
Mood										
Thought										
Activity										
Organ./Control										
Interpersonal										
Physical										

10–25 Within realm of expected behavior. Normal functioning. May want help with specific problems. Preventive therapy.

26–40 Serious stresses and problems. Professional help may be advisable. Functioning with difficulty.

40–50 Marginal functioning. Seek professional help.

4
····

Test Interpretation and Evaluation

INTERPRETATION

For general interpretation, your point scores and bar graph can be broken down to one of three possible categories. A score in the *10 to 25 point range* is within the realm of *expected normal behavior and normal functioning*. You may want help with specific problems and might benefit from preventive therapy, but you have no serious mental or emotional problems at this time and you have a high level of mental adaptability.

If you score in the *26 to 40 point range,* you are *functioning, but with difficulty.* You have serious stresses and problems, and professional help is probably advisable.

A score in the *40 to 50 point range* indicates the level of *marginal functioning* and is a clear call to seek professional help.

Once again, remember that your mental health changes over time, as does your physical health. Whatever category of mental adaptability you may be in today is not necessarily a permanent definition of your mental well-being. At the same time, be aware that your mental health might possibly deteriorate rather than improve, if problems are left untreated. A healthy environment or positive intervention might greatly increase your sense of well-being.

SELF-EVALUATION

The bar graph gives you a picture of your overall emotional well-being. It tells you which areas of behavior give you problems, the degree to which they are problems, and the areas in which you are functioning well. Note that very few scores will fall in either the normal category of 10 to 15 points, or the severe disorder category of 45 to 50 points. Most scores and most people fall somewhere in between. We all have mental problems of varying degrees, but we are still able to function.

Depending on your bar graph scores, the state of your mental health may be obvious at a glance or, for borderline cases, you may need a more precise point evaluation. The calculation of an exact point score is possible. Merely add up your point scores for each of the seven characteristics and divide by seven as in the following examples.

SAMPLE SCORES, INTERPRETATION, AND DISCUSSION

CASE ONE: A Borderline Normal Person

Mental Health Bar Graph

POINT SCORES		NORMAL	DIFFICULTIES	MARGINAL
		10 15 20 25	30 35 40	45 50
Tension	24			
Mood	19			
Thought	27			
Activity	16			
Organ./Control	10			
Interpersonal	30			
Physical	42			
Total score	168			
divided by 7 = 24				

THE GRAPH SHOWS, AS DOES THE POINT SCORE, THAT
THIS PERSON HAS A BORDERLINE NORMAL STATE OF
MENTAL HEALTH.

Interpretation
- This person exhibits minor problems in tension behavior, minimal problems with mood and activity, and excellent organization/control behavior.
- There are major problems in thought and interpersonal behavior and extremely serious physical problems.
- Except for physical behavior, no other category exceeds anxious coping behavior; therefore, Case One is best regarded as *borderline normal.*
- It would be wise to investigate the physical problems, which in this case would appear to be caused as much by the physical as the mental factors.
- The excellent organization/control score indicates strong inner reserves, self-discipline, and the capacity to overcome your problems.

Suggestions
- This person should seek attention for physical problems. As a minimum, he or she should have a physical checkup, watch diet, and follow a routine of regular exercise.
- For interpersonal problems, this person should seek informal or short-term counseling, or possibly group therapy. (Informal refers to individual counseling with a pastor or someone who is not formally trained or licensed, or with a support group led by someone who is not licensed.)

CASE TWO: An Extremely Adaptable Person

Mental Health Bar Graph

POINT SCORES		NORMAL		DIFFICULTIES		MARGINAL
		10 15 20	25 30 35	40 45 50		
Tension	15					
Mood	10					
Thought	10					
Activity	15					
Organ./Control	10					
Interpersonal	12					
Physical	18					
Total score	90					

divided by 7 = 12.9

THE GRAPH SHOWS, AS DOES THE POINT SCORE, THAT THIS PERSON HAS A NORMAL STATE OF MENTAL HEALTH.

Interpretation
- An enviable score. No major emotional problems. Some minor physical problems, and an occasional symptom in tension behavior and activities.

Suggestions
- This person is very fortunate. No changes in lifestyle are indicated.

CASE THREE: A Person with Major Emotional Problems

Mental Health Bar Graph

POINT SCORES		NORMAL		DIFFICULTIES		MARGINAL
		10 15 20	25 30 35	40 45 50		
Tension	35					
Mood	25					
Thought	25					
Activity	40					
Organ./Control	33					
Interpersonal	45					
Physical	35					
Total score	238					

divided by 7 = 34

THE GRAPH SHOWS, AS DOES THE POINT SCORE, THAT THIS PERSON HAS MAJOR EMOTIONAL PROBLEMS, BORDERING BETWEEN STAGE THREE (ANXIOUS COPING) AND STAGE FOUR (ANXIOUS CHARACTER).

Interpretation
- This is a clear case in which intervention would be advisable. A score of 34 indicates severe interpersonal problems that should receive immediate attention.
- All areas are subject to problems, although mood and thought behavior are still more or less under control.
- A person with this score is still functioning, but with great difficulties and great stress.

Suggestions
- This person would probably benefit from some form of professional guidance.
- His or her problems are greater than those normally encountered. It might be very helpful to treat them before they get worse.

CASE FOUR: A Normal Person with Minor Problems

Mental Health Bar Graph

POINT SCORES		NORMAL	DIFFICULTIES	MARGINAL
		10 15 20	25 30 35 40	45 50
Tension	15			
Mood	22			
Thought	20			
Activity	20			
Organ./Control	24			
Interpersonal	20			
Physical	15			
Total score	136			
divided by 7 = 19.4				

THE GRAPH SHOWS, AS DOES THE POINT SCORE, THAT THIS IS A NORMAL PERSON WITH MANY MINOR EMOTIONAL PROBLEMS.

Interpretation

• A point score of 19.4 indicates a person within the range of normal behavior, but approximating to stage two, state-of-alert behavior.

• If a real state of alert exists, these symptoms are perfectly normal and the external factors should be altered, rather than the subject be treated.

• If external conditions are normal and no state of alert exists, then these symptoms may indicate more significant mental problems and should receive treatment. Most people with this score, however, are merely suffering from the normal stresses and difficulties of daily living in an imperfect world.

Suggestions

• This person's general mental health is good, but he or she should take care regarding mood and organization/control behavior.

• The organization/control score indicates problems in self-control and self-discipline and is a probable danger signal indicating a need for at least some informal attention to this aspect of this person's life.

• Depending on other factors, no immediate action is necessary. If this person has misgivings about the direction of his or her life, he or she might seek enrichment or preventive therapy in some form (anything from meditation to a self-help group, or a therapy group in accordance with their personality).

• This person has problems, but they are not interfering with normal functioning.

Other Important Tests and Quick Tips

....

5
. . . .

"Check Your Stress" Test

Now that you've taken and scored yourself on our Test of Adaptability, we'd like to help you look at your emotional well-being from a slightly different point of view. The "Check Your Stress" Test, also known as the Life Change Index Scale and the Holmes and Rahe Social Re-adjustment Rating Scale, looks at the stress in your life. It is based on the theory that change, even positive change, causes stress and that different kinds of change produce different amounts of stress. The fact that stress induced by life changes can cause physical illness as well as emotional problems has been studied and well documented.

This test will help you to quantify the amount and types of change you've experienced in the past 12 months. The items in the test fall into two categories: ones that reflect your personal lifestyle—choices over which you have some control; and ones that reflect events or occurrences that happen *to you*, for which you have less control. We think you'll find the test both interesting and illuminating.

THE "CHECK YOUR STRESS" TEST[1]

(The Life Change Index Scale)
by Thomas H. Holmes and Richard H. Rahe

To help you identify some of the stresses in your life, the following scale cites positive and negative life events. Each is rated according to the amount of adjustment needed to cope with them. To use the scale, add up the scores for the life changes you have experienced within the past year and place the total on the line at the end of the scale.

1	Death of spouse	1	____	100
2	Divorce	2	____	73
3	Marital separation from mate	3	____	65
4	Detention in jail or other institution	4	____	63
5	Death of a close family member	5	____	63
6	Major personal injury or illness	6	____	53
7	Marriage	7	____	60
8	Being fired at work	8	____	47
9	Marital reconciliation	9	____	45
10	Retirement from work	10	____	45
11	Major change in health or behavior of a family member	11	____	44
12	Pregnancy	12	____	40
13	Sexual difficulties	13	____	39
14	Gaining a new family member (e.g., through birth, adoption, oldster moving in, etc.)	14	____	39
15	Major business readjustment (e.g., merger, reorganization, bankruptcy, etc.)	15	____	38
16	Major change in financial state (e.g., either a lot worse off or a lot better off than usual)	16	____	37
17	Death of a close friend	17	____	36
18	Changing to a different line of work	18	____	36
19	Major change in the number of arguments with spouse (e.g., either a lot			

	more or a lot less than usual regarding child-rearing, personal habits, etc.)	19	____	25
20	Taking on a mortgage greater than $10,000 (e.g., purchasing a home, business, etc.)	20	____	31
21	Foreclosure on a mortgage or loan	21	____	30
22	Major change in responsibilities at work (e.g., promotion, demotion, lateral transfer)	22	____	29
23	Son or daughter leaving home (e.g., marriage, attending college, etc.)	23	____	29
24	In-law troubles	24	____	29
25	Outstanding personal achievement	25	____	28
26	Spouse beginning or ceasing work outside the home	26	____	26
27	Beginning or ceasing formal schooling	27	____	26
28	Major change in living conditions (e.g., building a new home, remodeling, deterioration of home or neighborhood)	28	____	25
29	Revision of personal habits (dress, manners, associations, etc.)	29	____	24
30	Troubles with the boss	30	____	23
31	Major change in working hours or conditions	31	____	20
32	Change in residence	32	____	20
33	Changing to a new school	33	____	20
34	Major change in usual type and/or amount of recreation	34	____	19
35	Major change in church activities (e.g., a lot more or a lot less than usual)	35	____	19
36	Major change in social activities (e.g., clubs, dancing, movies, visiting, etc.)	36	____	18
37	Taking on a mortgage or loan less than $10,000 (e.g., purchasing a car, TV, freezer, etc.)	37	____	17
38	Major change in sleeping habits (a lot more or a lot less sleep or change in time of day when asleep)	38	____	16
39	Major change in number of family get-togethers (e.g., a lot more or a lot less than usual)	39	____	15

40	Major change in eating habits (a lot more or a lot less food intake, or very different meal hours or surroundings)	40	_____	15
41	Vacation	41	_____	13
42	Christmas	42	_____	12
43	Minor violations of the law (e.g., traffic tickets, jaywalking, disturbing the peace. etc.)	43	_____	11

Total Life Change Units (LCU) _____

Interpreting Your Score

0–150   Your score indicates no significant problem. You have a manageable level of stress in your life.

150–199   You are in the *Mild Life Crisis Level* with a 35 percent chance of illness. You need to be aware of the sources of stress in your life.

200–299   You are in the *Moderate Life Crisis Level* with a 50 percent chance of illness. You need to reduce your stress as soon as possible.

300 plus You are in the *Major Life Crisis Level* with an 80 percent chance of illness. You need to seriously reevaluate your life and immediately reduce further risks to your health.

HOW DID YOU DO?

Were there any big surprises for you? Did you appreciate that all of these changes, even the positive events, add up to so many points?

The test may help you to put your life in perspective. We hope that you can get a concrete view of the actual sources of stress in your life and that you can make the necessary adjustments. None of us can ever have total control over our choices or the events in our lives (nor would we want to), but we do have partial control and therefore we have partial responsibility for the quality of our lives. Having a sense of balance and control in your life is part of achieving good mental health.

Also, you might be surprised to learn that there can be a long (two years or more) delay between stress-producing events and the eventual illness, if the stress is not relieved in some way. Stress-producing events are not always dramatic, but they are cumulative. Stress-related symptoms can also be subtle, especially at first. Stress can cause many physical problems. Common complaints include headaches, stomachaches, heartburn, constipation, diarrhea, shoulder and back pain, chest pain, insomnia, etc. Psychological effects of stress can also sneak up on you gradually. These include difficulty concentrating, difficulty making decisions, frequent crying, fatigue, anger, depression, and impotency. You cannot assume that these symptoms are caused by stress; see your doctor in order to rule out other possible causes.

Finally, we must remember the words of Hans Selye, M.D., the father of modern stress research, "Complete freedom from stress is death." Some stress is a necessary part of life that cannot be avoided entirely. But, both too little or too much stress can lead to a state of *dis*-stress. It is distress (not stress alone) that sets the stage for mind/body *dis*-ease. Health is a matter of creating and maintaining a delicate balance.

6

Quick Tips for Improving Your Mental Health: Ten Transitional States and How to Cope with Them

Life is about change. We are continually experiencing change. Our ability to adapt is the cornerstone of mental health. The "Check Your Stress" test in Chapter 5 conveniently helps us to look at stress. It also leads us to look at 10 transitional states that are often associated with higher rates of emotional distress. These 10 categories of change give us additional information to help us understand our mental and emotional adaptability. Please note that these categories are not listed according to any numeric order of importance.

1. New Job, New School, New House

All *firsts* are potentially stressful. No matter how positive or desired the change is, there is always a high degree of anxiety associated with new beginnings. Will the job work out? Will co-workers accept me? Will I make new friends at school and perform adequately? Will I and my children adjust to the new house and neighborhood? Change is exhilarating, but it also creates doubt and anxiety when we leave our old well-established comfort zones and venture into the new and unknown.

Quick Tip #1 If we accept that life is about change, then we must accept that some degree of stress is also a *necessary* part of life. If we embrace change and adapt ourselves both mentally and emotionally, we can be better prepared. It is important to adjust your expectations realistically when you embark on a new journey. You may even have to lower your normal standards temporarily. If we are unnecessarily demanding and perfectionistic, our journey becomes difficult and joyless. Do you allow room for error in yourself, in your loved ones, and in new situations? Or, are you rigid, tense, and intolerant of mistakes? Can you laugh at yourself and others? *She who laughs lasts.*

We all need to consider a basic philosophic question: Is life a struggle to be overcome or an experience to be savored? When you go through a major new experience, you need to allow for a period of "rough edges" where you can adjust yourself through creating reasonable and appropriate expectations. Being good to yourself and those around you is a sign of positive mental health!

2. Gain or Loss of a Love Partner

The gain of a love partner is certainly wonderful, but definitely stressful. Added to the problem of newness are two other disruptive factors. First is the reaction of those to whom you are currently close, including your family and friends. A new partner is bound to affect your existing social circle.

In addition, there may be personality clashes, disapproval, or just a required rearrangement of your prior habits and activities. There is also the fear of loss, which accompanies all new relationships; it is not necessarily rational or conscious, but it still exists. Jealousy, possessiveness, and obsessive devotion are all possible manifestations of this fear of loss of a new love partner. Finally, the loss of someone you once loved through divorce or separation can be an extreme hazard to your mental health. Couples who have lived together for years face the additional trauma of trying to rebuild an entire life with new sets of friends, new activities, and new roles as single persons. Such changes are difficult to handle at any time, but they are especially difficult when combined with grief and mourning. Note item #19 on the "Check Your Stress" test; even a change in the number of arguments with a spouse can be a significant stressor.

Quick Tip #2 If you're beginning a marriage or a new relationship, please consider that research shows that the first year of living together can be very stressful. As the honeymoon period wanes, each partner gets a more realistic view of the actual strengths, weaknesses, and human quirks of their partner. This is generally a very necessary adjustment in all relationships and is to be expected. You need a sense of humor and play and the correct mental attitude: *Isn't this person fascinating? Isn't it interesting how we are going to work things out and resolve our differences?* As differences emerge in opinions, in tastes, and in human needs, you have an opportunity for sharing and for really getting to know each other. If either you or your partner bring children from a previous relationship into the marriage, you'll need to be even more patient and tolerant.

If you're coming out of a marriage or long-term relationship, you may need to mourn or grieve this loss. This is a very necessary stage for both men and women. Even if it was a bitter breakup and you are thrilled to be separated, there will be loss and memories of good times shared with your ex-mate. At times like this, you need real friends with whom to share your feelings and to relieve the sense of loss and loneliness. You may need to join a social group in order to involve yourself with people. Or, you may need to be alone for a period to reflect quietly and to review your situation. *Be kind to yourself.* You may feel confused, or down, or incapable of making big decisions, or even of cleaning your house. This is normal. This is usually a temporary state of mind, so give yourself permission to be in transition. Self-love means learning not to be too judgemental of oneself at times like these.

Accept your needs and beware of running around in a frenzy, madly trying to fill the empty void within. There is no need to be a macho man or macho woman, denying your true feelings. Separation hurts—accept the fact and be prepared to deal with it, and allow yourself a period for healing.

3. Physical Illness or Injury

Physical illnesses or injuries, especially of long duration, are likely to lead to emotional difficulties as well. Even minor colds can produce states of irritability and depression. Major illnesses often call for the abandonment of entire work, play, or love activities and an essential readjustment of all phases of your life. Particularly in American society, which puts a premium on independence and individual autonomy, it is difficult for adults to accept a dependent and passive role.

Quick Tip #3 Physical health and well-being is another basic cornerstone of mental health. If you have a physical problem, take care of it—visit a doctor and get the proper medical treatment. Please remember that many physical conditions can produce symptoms of emotional distress or worsen existing ones. For instance, thyroid problems can produce feelings of fatigue and can mimic feelings of depression that seem quite real. Similarly, Seasonal Affective Disorder (SAD) is a condition in which people often experience depression when they are deprived of enough direct contact with sunlight. These are two conditions that are very treatable if you go for help.

If you have a physical handicap or challenge, be prepared to deal with it through acceptance and proper mental attitude. Accepting limitations is a part of good mental health. This does not mean burying yourself under a rock; it means making the most of what you can do, compensating for losses, and finding new sources of pleasure.

4. Parenthood

Any problems a marriage may have had are likely to reappear with the birth of children. If value conflicts or misunderstandings about the goals of the marriage have not been worked through, they may create stresses at this time. Family changes such as pregnancy, gaining a new family member, or children leaving home are also sources of stress. Parenthood and family life produce some of life's greatest joys and deepest stresses.

Quick Tip #4 As Kahlil Gibran said, "Your children do not come from you, they pass through you." Children are mirrors for their parents. If we can deal with our children's problems with patience and acceptance, our children will draw strength from us. We will then be more effective as parents and happier as human beings. It also helps to see our children as separate from ourselves. They are not just extensions of ourselves. They do have lives of their own.

Each child is unique and has a deep need to be acknowledged and appreciated for his or her own particular strengths. All children need clear and consistent guidelines. Parents need to work together as a united team. Unresolved differences between parents need to be worked out quietly and away from children. If parents cannot resolve their differences, they need to agree to go for help, both for themselves and for the sake of their children's psychological health. Children have the right to grow up in a calm and nurturing environment. Going for marital counseling is not a sign of failure. It is a sign of maturity that two adults acknowledge that they need help from an impartial, trained outsider.

5. Marriage or Long-term Relationship

While marriage or long-term relationship may not seem to be a transition state, we include it in our list of potentially difficult passages. Let's face it, half of all marriages end in divorce. Fifty percent is a high statistic, and that figure cuts through almost all segments of our society. What does this say? It says that marriage has become a risky business. As an institution it may not have the same meaning for current generations as it did for our parents and grandparents.

Most people still marry with the stated intention of remaining in lifelong partnership. In reality, however, that model may no longer be the predominant one. Many people will be serially monogamous. They will have two or three serious relationships in the course of their lifetime, and they may have children with more than one of these partners. Many people are also rejecting traditional marriages; these couples may live together for either a short or long duration. We seem to have entered a brave new world, and no one is quite sure how it all will turn out. Nevertheless, marriage—in whatever form—is an enduring institution that seems destined to survive despite our attempts to modify it or escape from it.

Quick Tip #5 Every year books on love and marriage are at the top of the bestseller list. We seem to have an endless appetite for finding out what's gone wrong or for learning how to do it better. The plain truth is that love and intimacy have always been an ideal that is seldom reached and, at best, is difficult to maintain. In addition, we seem today to have much greater expectations and less patience than previous generations that stuck together "'til death do us part."

If you read all of the advice books, you would come away with one basic guideline: A good marriage is based on good communication, which requires a certain amount of quality contact over a period of time. This is necessary for establishing a sense of trust and togetherness. Sounds simple—why is it so difficult? We suggest the following ways for couples to achieve and maintain good communication:

1. The two most important times of the day for couples are perhaps the time preceding bedtime and the time of initial contact, when couples greet each other, such as upon arriving home after work. If couples were to simply establish these two periods as important 5-minute encounters, they would create the daily habit of loving contact and positive expectations. Modern life with its many distractions and stresses on both partners requires this simple bond for love to grow and to prosper. We would hope that your marriage

or relationship is worth the trouble to schedule these daily comfort zones.

2. Couples need to schedule one 15-minute meeting a week together. Just one. At these meetings they are to be alone, undistracted by television or children, and they are to discuss one simple question, "How are we doing?" Each partner might take a moment to become up-to-date, to clear the air, to share a grievance, or simply to express a moment of appreciation. This meeting is not to be confused with going out for the evening or having dinner together or with having sex. It is simply a personal relationship meeting.

Studies have shown that couples who can practice these two extraordinarily simple means of communication have a greater chance of building a bond and keeping it even during the tough times. It is amazing how many couples, including really bright, otherwise successful people, can't manage to grasp the importance of these daily and weekly meetings! These same people run businesses and are often community leaders, but somehow the importance of this kind of meeting and bonding eludes them. It takes about 5 to 10 percent more effort and patience to create a good or a great marriage than to endure a difficult one. You could put these simple principles into practice now, in your own creative way; or you could wait until you go for marital counseling. Hopefully, you will see that these small changes may enhance your marriage or relationship.

Finally, good communication may be aided by marital counseling, which, by the way, is usually short-term and an excellent investment of time and money. Couples usually learn the crucial skills of listening, articulating their needs, and negotiating and expressing their emotions. Some of these same skills may also be learned in "marriage enrichment" or "marriage encounter" programs sponsored by various churches and other organizations. *It takes time and effort to learn the language of love and relationships. Do you have the time and the desire?*

What's Your M.Q. (Marriage Quotient)?

The 7 Deadly Sins
How to Make a
Miserable Marriage:

1. Be reactive to your mate's every word or glance.
2. Wait for your mate to initiate loving or caring behavior.
3. Remind your mate often of all of their worst shortcomings.
4. Always assume the worst and talk in an accusing tone; when you fight dredge up everything from the past.
5. Talk only when there's a crisis or problem. Generally sulk, withdraw and act hurt.
6. Generally expect the worst and remain hopeless, angry, or depressed.
7. Above all, make sure to wait for your mate to change first, before you make any change in your own behavior.

The 7 Golden Steps
How to Make a Good
Marriage (Or Intimate
Relationship):

1. Be flexible, open, positive, or neutral in relation to your mate.
2. Be loving for the pleasure of being loving whether your mate responds or not.
3. Learn to value and acknowledge your mate's good qualities and let them know it.
4. If you must fight, be specific and learn to fight fair and clean—stay in the present.
5. Be willing to talk, to listen, and to negotiate.
6. Take the time to develop shared interests and values.
7. Be content to work on changing yourself, whether your mate follows suit or not.

Q: Do You Need an Attitude Adjustment?

It takes about the same time and energy to create a good or bad marriage.

6. Career and Financial Changes

Work constitutes a large part of adult life for most men and women today. Accordingly, changing jobs, getting fired or promoted, changing your career or job responsibilities, being unemployed, or retiring can all be sources of stress. Similarly, changes in your finances for better and for worse can be unsettling, as are home purchases, mortgages, and foreclosures. There is no doubt about it, changes in work and financial status will make you vulnerable to physical and emotional upsets.

Quick Tip #6 Money and how you manage it is also a reflection of your overall mental health and emotional maturity. It is, of course, a necessary part of life. It is also something to learn about and to become comfortable with. *How is your fiscal fitness?* If you have continual problems with finances, you will also undoubtedly have physical stresses and emotional difficulties. Is your stomach tied up in knots? Are you losing sleep over money problems? A sign of maturity is when you stop blaming "life" and "other people" and begin to acknowledge that *you* need help. It makes good sense to reach out for help in order to regain control over your life and your finances.

Fortunately, you are not alone if you have problems with money. Literally hundreds of thousands of people take advantage of free or low-cost services such as the Consumer Credit Counseling Services and Debtor's Anonymous. These organizations exist solely for the purpose of helping people to bring order and clarity into their financial lives. They will even assist you in creating a budget if necessary. Because finances are an important part of mental health, we list these organizations in Appendix C.

7. Adolescence

The "Check Your Stress" test is geared to adults, but adolescence in itself can become a cause for concern. In adolescence the often cited "identity crisis" appears as the young person asks, Who am I and who will I become? An adolescent experiences rapid unprecedented changes—physical, hormonal, mental, and emotional—*all at the same time.* In adolescence each decision appears to be momentous, as if it is the key to the youth's entire future. Studies show that this is a particularly difficult period of life for both the child and the parents, who must guide their child through this period of change and strong emotions. Despite their protests and their requests for freedom, adolescents still need a lot of re-assurance and guidance.

Quick Tip #7 If you are prepared, you will survive your children's adolescence. If you are not, it will cause immeasurable strain on yourself and your marriage. At a time when you might wish to be more involved with other interests, you need to be actively involved in your teenager's growth and development. You need to learn to *listen,* and to interact calmly and deliberately, instead of just reacting to your teen's impulsive behavior. Your involvement and good rapport with your teenager will have big payoffs. It will also prevent a certain normal amount of acting-out and negative attention-seeking by the teen. Remember, there are times when you must set limits, hold children accountable, and set appropriate consequences for their misconduct. Your humor, patience, and good judgment will be tested repeatedly! It helps greatly to have the company and counsel of other parents of teenagers, to band together for mutual strength and support. "It takes a whole village to raise a child" is certainly still true today.

If your adolescent is involved in a serious problem, you need to address it firmly and fairly in a timely manner. It does not help you or your child to bury your head in the sand about problems such as drugs, alcohol, sexual promiscuity, and school truancy. Some teenagers will actually welcome the opportunity to go for counseling with an objective third party. Many will not welcome help or advice, and they need to be taken to family counseling. In family counseling the whole family acknowledges that they have a problem, not just the troubled teenager. Parents need to be able to say, There is a problem here and *we* need to go for help, and you must join us. In addition, parents sometimes need help through counseling or parenting classes in order to become more effective as parents.

8. Midlife for Women and Men

Perimenopause, the transition period from procreativity to the time when the menses cease (menopause), can be particularly difficult for women. Following menopause, they are faced with a new self-image and issues that range from a greater sense of biological freedom to no longer being able to bear children. They must adjust to major hormonal changes within their bodies, which on occasion can affect their emotional stability and their overall sense of well-being.

For most men, the physical and hormonal changes may not be quite as stressful at midlife as they are for women. Men may have to readjust their lifestyle to match diminishing energy and physical prowess. More important, however, many men need to learn to develop new social skills and friendships with other men. Regrettably, a lot of men still lean on their wives and girlfriends as sole emotional support.

Quick Tip #8 Many new medical treatments and options are available for women who are having difficulties with perimenopause and with other problems of midlife. Women need to educate themselves about hormonal changes in their bodies, investigate estrogen replacement therapy, and actively reach out for information and support in making important health decisions in this phase of life.

In the last 25 years, there has been an explosion of women's health-care centers and women's support and self-help groups. Professional and informal peer support is available, often for free or for modest fees. Women who have medical and emotional problems at this time of life need to accept the inevitable changes and adjust their attitudes and their lifestyles. Studies show that women over 40 are actually happier and more confident and relaxed as they grow into their mature identities. Aging can be a beautiful experience for women. They no longer need to feel constrained and bound by old stereotypes and gender limitations. Women may need to find new role models as they journey through this exciting phase.

For men, midlife (somewhere between age 35 and 50) is a time of surrendering the grandiose fantasies of youth and accepting some choices that have already been made. Accepting existing "realities" in your career, health, geographic location, life-mate and family, can at first seem very limiting. Witness the popularity of the movie, "City Slickers," with Billy Crystal, where three aging buddies seek to escape midlife responsibilities and to regain some of the passion and adventure of their carefree youth.

The answer, of course, as the movie suggests, lies in finding and channeling some of the passion of one's youth into adult choices that make sense and can yield real rewards (both economic and emotional). At first this can seem quite depressing, but as men surrender the fantasies of youth, the real opportunities of midlife can open up in many areas. For many men it helps to begin to identify with peers and especially with older men rather than with the "younger generation." Finding successful older men (however *you* define success) as role models and as friends can be crucial. It can also be helpful to find support in men's groups where one can explore these issues with other men in a safe and sympathetic environment. Fortunately, there are now men's groups and men's centers in most U.S. cities. It is a growing trend that offers hope and concrete support, especially for men at midlife.

As the old roles continue to change, men are beginning to acknowledge the limits of competition and endless striving for money and achievement. Many now realize their worth goes beyond being providers. Men are often characterized as being bored or burnt out at midlife, but many are discovering new careers, new options, and new interests at this stage of life.

9. Old Age

Old age can be a uniquely challenging period of life. It is a transition state in the sense that men and women must adapt to ever-decreasing mental and physical energies and learn to accept less active and less independent roles, in the place of former active leadership roles in the family and at work. Older people face many tasks; they must begin to make peace with the lives they have lived, knowing that they cannot change the past, nor hope for some future changes to justify current losses or regrets. They must also accept inevitable death and resolve to live despite the loss of friends and the disappearance of most of what gave their lives meaning and fulfillment in their youth and middle age.

In addition, for some, as aging progresses, brain cells die, creating a variety of mental difficulties that range from mild senility to delusion, dementia, and other forms of confusion. Deafness, blindness, and illnesses requiring or resulting in social isolation and confinement produce conditions ripe for the outbreak of insecurity, anxiety, and other stresses, which in turn lead to mental disturbances. Remarkably, despite these problems, people are now living longer, healthier, and more productive lives well into their eighties and nineties.

Quick Tip #9 Much has been written about aging, and much research is still needed. Studies do show, however, that personality does not change so much over time. At age 80, an adult's basic personality is relatively the same as it was at age 30. While our bodies change, our inner being seems to have a life of its own.

As a nation we are rapidly aging. We need to learn to value older people as national resources for love and wisdom and as good role models. One of the greatest dangers of aging is the loss of self-esteem based on the loss of productivity and normal physical changes. Older men and women need knowledge and information, especially about improving their health, their finances, and their social lives. If possible, it helps to plan for retirement many years in advance. They will need to find new sources of pleasure that are appropriate to this stage of life. This may include finding new activities, new housing, and new friends in order to make the most of the retirement years.

Regardless of their previous status, older people need to be able to adapt to changing conditions and circumstances. It requires great courage at any age to overcome lifetime habits and a sense of pride in order to reach out for help. Seniors vary greatly in their overall status and in their personal ambitions, but all of them, regardless of their differences, must find a sense of purpose and reasons for living. Studies show that those who are engaged in their interests and relationships do live longer, healthier, and more fulfilled lives.

10. Death

The deaths of friends, lovers, parents, and family members are difficult moments in which to maintain mental adaptability. All human cultures have evolved elaborate rituals of mourning to ease the pain and mental anguish for those who survive the death of intimates. Death is doubly traumatic. First, it brings into play all the disturbing factors associated with the loss of a love partner. Second, new patterns of living must follow the loss of significant people in your life, and new adjustments and identifications of yourself must also be made. Daily life won't be the same after the loss of a parent or close friend.

Death, in and of itself, is probably the most disturbing fact of life. When close friends or family members die, something within us dies as well. Fortunately, what remains are our memories, images, feelings, and shared experiences. Inevitably, death questions our most fundamental assumption about ourselves and our lives.

Quick Tip #10 Mourning is a perfectly natural and normal part of life. There are many small losses in life, but none truly prepare us for the loss of a loved one. It is important to accept the loss by allowing yourself to actually experience it. There is a tendency to go numb or to block the painful feelings associated with death. Many traditional cultures are actually more adept than ours at providing elaborate rituals to help people to accept the deaths of loved ones.

America is a mix of many cultures, but is young as a nation and as a civilization. We are slowly coming to accept death as a necessary fact of life. It is no longer a hidden or taboo topic as it was one generation ago. It helps greatly, of course, to have friends and relatives to talk to and lean on for emotional and concrete support, especially after a death. It is also a tremendous support if you have a religious or spiritual faith, or a belief system that will sustain you through difficult times.

To overcome the sense of isolation and silence, it helps to have friends who have also experienced death and who know how to console you. Some people are unable to grieve a death and are unable to continue to live a functioning life. They need to be able to reach out for professional help or to go to grief groups. Most communities have groups for widows, widowers, children, parents, and others who are struggling with the loss of a loved one. (Churches and synagogues are often a good place to find out about these important groups).

7

Are You
Depressed?

Depression is one of the most common and treatable of all mental illnesses. In any six-month period, 9.4 million Americans suffer from this illness. One in 4 women and 1 in 10 men can expect to develop it during their lifetime. *Eighty to 90 percent of those who suffer from depression can be effectively treated.*

We all get "the blues," but are you *depressed*? The self-test on the next page can help you find out whether you suffer from serious depression.

ARE YOU DEPRESSED?[2]
A Self Test

	YES	NO
1. I feel downhearted and sad.	____	____
2. I don't enjoy the things I used to do.	____	____
3. I have felt so low that I've thought of suicide.	____	____
4. I feel that I am not useful or needed.	____	____
5. I notice I am losing weight.	____	____
6. I have trouble sleeping through the night.	____	____
7. I am restless and can't keep still.	____	____
8. My mind isn't as clear as it used to be.	____	____
9. I get tired for no reason.	____	____
10. I feel hopeless about the future.	____	____

HOW TO RATE YOUR TEST

You may be suffering from serious depression if you answered Yes to at least five questions, *and* you answered Yes to either Question 1 or Question 2 *and* these symptoms have persisted for at least two weeks. *Regardless of your test results, if you answered Yes to Question 3, you should seek professional help immediately.*

THE ZUNG SELF-RATING DEPRESSION SCALE

The test you just took is a shorter version of the Zung Self-Rating Depression Scale, a very widely used and well-respected test.

If this test stimulated your interest you might wish to

know about the National Depression Screening Day Project. Each year in October during Mental Illness Awareness Week, this national association provides *free* screening for depression at thousands of sites across the country. In 1993, 56,000 people attended these screenings where they learned about depression, were given a confidential written screening test, and discussed results with a medical health professional, all on the same day.

Nearly 1,500 persons were sufficiently depressed that they were considered to be at risk for suicide and were referred for help. This represented a potential saving of 1,500 lives. If you feel continually downhearted and sad, find it hard to work or make decisions, or simply do not enjoy your life, you may be one of more than 18 million Americans who suffer from depression each year. You or someone you know may wish to contact this association. (See National Depression Screening Day Project in Appendix C.)

THE BIG D—WHAT'S IT ALL ABOUT?

Often called the "common cold of mental illness," depression is not to be confused with feeling sad, having "the blues," or just feeling down. We all have "low" periods where we feel discouraged, especially during difficult times. This is very normal, and usually these feelings will soon pass. But a person who cannot "snap out of it" or get over these feeling within two weeks may be suffering from real clinical depression.

Depression can occur at *any* age. People suffering from depression have pervasive feelings of sadness—they feel down almost all of the time. For some it's like a feeling in their bones, for others it's like a heavy cloud that constantly surrounds them. Depressed people may feel helpless, hopeless, and irritable. They may also have real problems with sleeping or eating, and they may feel tired or exhausted much of the time. They may have trouble working or relating to people.

There are many kinds of depression, and much research has been done in determining some of the causes of depression (genetic, chemical, biological, and environmental factors). The good news is that depression is very treatable and very reversible regardless of the type or cause of the depression. Many sophisticated new medications have been developed since the 1950s.

Psychiatrists and medical doctors usually conduct a thorough evaluation in order to determine whether or not a person is depressed. During an evaluation a psychiatrist will include a medical/psychiatric history outlining a person's physical and emotional background and family history. A mental status exam is given, which includes a series of questions to determine a person's mood, thoughts, patterns of speech and memory, and any other manifestations of depression. A physical exam may also be required. Doctors can then choose from a very wide range of effective medications to help the depressed person.

Some form of psychotherapy or counseling may be recommended in addition to medication, or even instead of medication for many individuals. Many kinds of "talk" therapies and other therapies are useful in the treatment of depression. *Cognitive behavioral therapy* uses various techniques of talk therapy and behavioral prescriptions to alleviate negative thoughts and beliefs. *Psychoanalysis* is an intensive form of treatment that helps patients to relieve depression based on conflicts from the past. These patients meet with their therapists three to five times a week. *Psychodynamic psychotherapy* is a less intense form of therapy (patients meet only once or twice a week) that helps patients develop insight into past and current conflicts, including their unconscious motivation. *Electroconvulsive therapy (ECT)* is a treatment that is used when other therapies have failed. It works by affecting the same transmitter chemicals in the brain that are affected by medications.

Regarding depression we might take a cue from President Franklin Delano Roosevelt who said, "There is nothing to fear but fear itself." Millions of Americans who have gone for help wonder why they had not sought help sooner.

PART

III
• • • •

Special Section
for Seniors

• • • •

8

Mental Health and the Elderly: A National Concern

DID YOU KNOW...?

Seniors currently account for 12 percent of our population; by the year 2020 they will comprise almost 20 percent, or one out of five Americans. Studies show that seniors are at greater risk of mental problems than are younger people. Having had good mental health throughout your life does not guarantee that you will have it in your senior years. From 13 to 25 percent of the elderly in the United States suffer from significant symptoms of mental illness and could benefit from help. Also, the highest rate of suicide in America is among those age 65 and older, accounting for 20 percent of all suicides nationwide.[3] *There is clearly a problem here.*

Sadly, most senior citizens do not seek help for mental and emotional problems—help that could alleviate their symptoms and return them to their previous level of functioning. *Why do they resist help?* Many older people don't understand the problems of mental health or acknowledge that they even exist. Many feel ashamed of their symptoms. Often, the patients, their loved ones and friends, and even their own doctors fail to recognize the symptoms of treatable mental illness in older people. They blame the symptoms on "old age" or think nothing can be done to alleviate the problem. This is simply not true. Even Medicare, which sets the standard for health-care insurance coverage, has traditionally discriminated against psychological care by having a low level of benefits.

This situation represents not only a terrible waste of human potential but also unnecessary pain and unhappiness. Who suffers as a result of these facts? Everyone. *Can we as a society turn this around?* Change begins with *you*.

9

....

The "Zest for Life" Test

Specifically designed for senior citizens, the "Zest for Life" Test (originally called the Life Satisfaction Inventory) is highly regarded as a measure of overall psychological well-being. It is a short, easy-to-use test that we hope you will find both interesting and informative. Designed by a team of psychologists (Neugarten, Havighurst, and Tobin) in 1961 as part of the Kansas City Study of Adult Life, the test was further refined by sociologist Dr. David L. Adams. It has been around a long time and continues to be highly respected by researchers and gerontologists.

We provide this test as simply another way of taking stock of your own strengths and weaknesses, *not* as a final decree of mental health. We encourage you to give it a chance and see if the test sheds light on your own situation and life experience. If it proves helpful or illuminating, great. If not, we applaud you for giving it a try. Remember, your ability to try new things demonstrates your flexibility, risk-taking ability, and resilience, which are all indicators of emotional health at any age.

Helpful Tip Many seniors have told us that taking this test along with a trusted friend or partner is very helpful. It is an opportunity to calmly review your life. The act of reflecting on your life and sharing it with a friend can be a very supportive and enriching experience. And it can be fun!

93

THE "ZEST FOR LIFE" TEST[4]

Here are some statements about life in general that people feel differently about. Please read each statement on the list, and if you agree with it, put a check mark in the space under "AGREE." If you do not agree with a statement, put a check mark in the space under "DISAGREE." If you are not sure one way or the other, put a check mark in the space under "UNSURE."

	AGREE	DISAGREE	UNSURE
1. As I grow older, things seem better than I thought they would be.	____	____	____
2. I have gotten more of the breaks in life than most of the people I know.	____	____	____
3. This is the dreariest time of my life.	____	____	____
4. I am just as happy as when I was younger.	____	____	____
5. My life could be happier than it is now.	____	____	____
6. These are the best years of my life so far.	____	____	____
7. Most of the things I do are boring or monotonous.	____	____	____
8. I expect some interesting and pleasant things to happen to me in the future.	____	____	____
9. I feel old and somewhat tired.	____	____	____
10. The things I do are as interesting to me as they ever were.	____	____	____

	AGREE	DISAGREE	UNSURE
11. As I look back on my life so far, I am fairly well satisfied.	____	____	____
12. I would not change my past life even if I could.	____	____	____
13. Compared to other people my age, I make a good appearance.	____	____	____
14. I have made plans for things I'll be doing a month or a year from now.	____	____	____
15. When I think back over my life, I didn't get most of the important things I wanted.	____	____	____
16. Compared to other people, I get down in the dumps too often.	____	____	____
17. I've gotten pretty much what I expected out of life.	____	____	____
18. In spite of what people say, the lot of the average person is getting worse, not better.	____	____	____

UNDERSTANDING THE "ZEST FOR LIFE" TEST

The questions were presented at random. We scrambled them so that you wouldn't know which categories you were marking, and to make you less self-conscious of your choices. The 18 test items that you have just checked off represent four categories of life satisfaction: mood, zest for life, agreement between desired and achieved goals, and resolve and fortitude. Each of these categories measures a different quality, and when taken together as a whole they are a measure of the fifth category, self-concept.

The following is a key to the test categories and how to score your answers. Note that the questions are now arranged to fit into the appropriate categories.

CATEGORY	QUESTION	HOW TO SCORE	
I. Mood	4.	A. If you answer *Agree* score 1 point.	___
	6.	B. If you answer *Agree* score 1 point.	___
	5.	C. If you answer *Disagree* score 1 point.	___
	3.	D. If you answer *Disagree* score 1 point.	___
	7.	E. If you answer *Disagree* score 1 point.	___
	16.	F. If you answer *Disagree* score 1 point.	___
II. Zest for Life	10.	G. If you answer *Agree* score 1 point.	___
	14.	H. If you answer *Agree* score 1 point.	___
	13.	I. If you answer *Agree* score 1 point.	___
	1.	J. If you answer *Agree* score 1 point.	___
	8.	K. If you answer *Agree* score 1 point.	___
	9.	L. If you answer *Disagree* score 1 point.	___
III. Goals: Desire vs. Achievement	11.	M. If you answer *Agree* score 1 point.	___
	12.	N. If you answer *Agree* score 1 point.	___
	17.	O. If you answer *Agree* score 1 point.	___

IV.	15.	P. If you answer *Disagree*	___
Resolve &		score 1 point.	
Fortitude	18.	Q. If you answer *Disagree*	___
		score 1 point.	
	2.	R. If you answer *Agree*	___
		score 1 point.	

V. Self-Concept = Total Score (Questions 1–18 combined)

Your Total Points   ___

Point Scores	Explanation
15–18	You're in great shape. Keep doing what you're doing.
10–14	You're in pretty good shape overall. Continue to concentrate on your strengths.
5–9	You may be having difficulties in "aging gracefully," and you may need additional help and support from others.
0–4	You may be at risk both physically and emotionally. You may need to seek informal and professional help for medical support and emotional assistance.

Understanding the Categories

There are no exact scores for these categories. Please rate yourself along a spectrum from high to low.

Category I measures mood tone. This refers to your basic mood. Are you generally happy and optimistic? Do you use positive terms when referring to people and things? Do you take pleasure in life or are you generally depressed, lonely, or blue? Are you often bitter, irritable, or angry?

Category II measures your zest for life versus apathy. This refers to your enthusiasm of response to life and to your degree of involvement with activities, persons, or ideas. It doesn't matter whether you are involved alone or with others, whether these are socially approved activities, or whether they give you status. A person who loves to sit at home and knit rates just as high as a person who loves to get out and meet people. What counts is simply your passion. Lower ratings are given for apathy and boredom and involvement in meaningless activities.

Category III measures agreement between your desired and achieved goals. This refers to the degree to which you feel you have achieved your goals in life, whatever they may be. What counts is feeling you've accomplished whatever *you* think is important. High ratings go not only to someone who says, "I've managed to keep out of jail" but also to someone who says, "I've managed to send all of my kids to college." Lower ratings go to individuals who feel they have missed most of their opportunities, or who say, "I've never been suited to my work." Also low on the spectrum are those who want to be "loved" but merely feel "approved of." (*Note:* Regret for your lack of education is not considered significant, because it is unfortunately a universal response of all people except those who have attained high social status.)

Category IV measures personal resolve and fortitude. This refers to the extent to which you accept personal responsibility for your life. The opposite would be to feel resigned, to merely condone, or to passively accept what life has brought you. Do you accept your life as meaningful and inevitable? Are you relatively unafraid of death? Whether or not you have been a person of high initiative, do you accept resolutely and positively what life has brought you, or not? A person who felt life was a series of hard knocks but stood up to them would get a high rating. Lower ratings would include people who blame themselves too much and those who place blame on others or the world for their own failures and disappointments.

Category V is the measure of self-concept. Your total score is an overall measure of your life satisfaction and includes all of the previous four categories. This refers to your concept of yourself—your physical as well as your psychological and social attributes. You might say this is a combination of your self-acceptance, your self-identity, and your self-confidence. High ratings usually go to those who are concerned with grooming and appearance, who think of themselves as wise or mellow, who are comfortable in giving advice to others, who are proud of their accomplishments, who feel deserving of the good breaks they had, and who feel important to someone else. Lower ratings are scored by those who feel "old," weak, sick, or incompetent; those who feel themselves to be a burden to others; and those who speak disparagingly of themselves or of older people in general.

Congratulations, you've completed the "Zest for Life" Test. Whatever your score, be kind to yourself. Aging gracefully, whatever that means to you personally, is an art and a state of mind.

10

••••

Alzheimer's Disease

A lzheimer's disease is a progressive disorder of the brain that slowly kills nerve cells in the brain. This illness affects 4 million Americans today. It affects primarily people over 65, but can strike people in their forties and fifties. At least 1 in 20 adults age 65 and older suffers from this disease and almost half of those over 85 have this condition.

Alzheimer's disease usually has a gradual onset. Persons with this illness may experience confusion, memory loss, personality and behavioral changes, impaired judgment, and difficulty finding words, finishing thoughts, or following directions. Eventually, the disease leaves its victims unable to care for themselves.

Please beware: Having one or more of these symptoms is not a sure sign of Alzheimer's disease. We hope the following charts will help you to distinguish the normal signs of aging from the more troubling symptoms. The information presented in this chapter is not intended to scare you but to keep you up to date. Knowledge can go a long way in dispelling fears and in helping you to keep things in perspective.

FORGETFULNESS—WHEN IS IT NORMAL, WHEN IS IT A SYMPTOM?[5]

Forgetfulness isn't always the first sign of Alzheimer's disease. Most often, a person with Alzheimer's disease develops abrupt and uncharacteristic mood swings. However, memory loss can interefere with business, social, or family life so it makes people realize they need medical attention.

What is normal memory loss of aging, and what is an abnormal loss that may indicate Alzheimer's disease or some other condition that may or may not be reversible? The comparisons in the table on page 102 may help.

Anyone who suspects that a loved one may be suffering from Alzheimer's disease should not jump to conclusions too quickly. Many other illnesses mimic Alzheimer's disease (A.D.). Physicians must rule out these treatable conditions before making a correct diagnosis. They include:[6]

- *Depression.* Many symptoms of depression can look like A.D., such as unexplained fatigue, loss of energy, loss of appetite, sleeping disturbances, tension, anxiety, irritability, boredom, poor attention and concentration, feelings of worthlessness and helplessness, even thoughts of suicide. Remember, depression is common in the elderly and very treatable.

- *Reactions to medications;* drug interactions.

- *Chemical imbalances* caused by poor nutrition, pernicious anemia (vitamin B_{12} deficiency), or diabetes; imbalances of sodium or calcium; decreased or increased thyroid levels.

- *Heart and lung problems* that deprive the brain of adequate nutrition and oxygen.

- *Head injuries from falls;* exposure to environmental pollutants (lead, mercury, carbon monoxide, some pesticides and industrial pollutants); chronic alcoholism or meningitis. Dementias arising from many of these causes are also very serious and sometimes irreversible.

YOUNG ADULT TO RETIREMENT	ELDERLY PERSON	PERSON WITH ALZHEIMER'S
Is seldom forgetful	Forgets parts of an experience (e.g., can remember eating but doesn't remember what fruit was served at lunch)	Often forgets entire experiences (e.g., may not remember eating and demands a meal)
Remembers later	Often remembers later	Rarely remembers later
Acknowledges memory lapses lightly	Acknowledges lapses readily, often with a request for help in recalling information	Acknowledges lapses grudgingly after initial denial and attempts to compensate for lapse
Maintains skills, such as reading words or music	Skills usually remain intact	Skills deteriorate
Follows written or spoken directions easily	Usually able to to follow directions	Increasingly unable to follow directions
Can use notes or reminders	Usually able to use notes or reminders	Increasingly unable to use notes or reminders
Can care for self	Usually able to care for self	Increasingly unable to care for self

Not all dementias are caused by A.D. Brain damage caused by impaired circulation—called multi-infarct dementia—causes between 12 and 20 percent of dementia in older people. Parkinson's, Huntington's, and Creutfeldt-Jakob diseases also cause progressive dementia.

Our final checklist for Alzheimer's disease is an important one, but again please note that *even the presence of any or all of these symptoms is not a sure indicator of Alzheimer's disease.*

CHECKLIST OF ALZHEIMER'S DISEASE SYMPTOMS: 7 WARNING SIGNS[7]

____ 1. Loss of short-term memory occurs; a person can't learn new information.

____ 2. Loss of long-term memory occurs; a person can't remember personal information, such as birthplace or occupation.

____ 3. Judgment is impaired.

____ 4. Aphasia develops; a person can't recall words or understand the meaning of common words.

____ 5. Apraxia develops; a person loses control over his or her muscles and can't, for example, button shirts or operate zippers.

____ 6. Loss of spatial abilities; a person can't assemble blocks, arrange sticks in a certain order, or copy a three-dimensional figure.

____ 7. Personality changes; a person may become unusually angry, irritable, quiet, or confused.

WHAT TO DO AND WHERE TO GO

If you are concerned, your first step is to find a physician who knows and understands the elderly. This doctor could be a primary care physician, a neurologist, or a psychiatrist. There is no single diagnostic test for Alzheimer's disease. Physicians and psychiatrists will only give a diagnosis of probable Alzheimer's disease *after* a thorough medical, psychiatric, and neurological evaluation has ruled out other possible conditions. At a modern medical center, clinical diagnosis consists of a comprehensive battery of tests that can be quite accurate.

Much progress is being made today to help relieve the suffering of Alzheimer's patients and their families. We can only hope that research will continue to produce a better understanding and more effective treatments. For more information, see Organizations for Senior Citizens in Appendix C.

Final note: If you were able to follow this chapter, you probably don't have Alzheimer's disease. Relax, take a deep breath and continue to move on to the next chapter.

Ten Steps to Improve Your Mind and Reduce the Risk of Alzheimer's

R ecent studies at Harvard and Columbia Universities and in France, all involving thousands of seniors have found that if you are mentally active you can reduce the risk of Alzheimer's disease or senility.[8] You don't have to be highly educated or in an intellectual occupation, but *you must use your mind, preferably in new or stimulating ways.*

1. *Start a new or challenging hobby.* It could be sewing, bridge, chess, photography, or anything that encourages you to focus on an outside interest where you sharpen your intellect.

2. *Reading is good for you.* Read any kind of material that engages you and enlivens your mind.

3. *Go to community events.* Interact with other people with similar interests; attend readings given by local authors at bookstores and libraries; attend local theaters and community college classes.

4. *Help other people.* By helping others in your community you feel useful, stimulated, and more upbeat. It's good for you!

5. *Keep in touch with family and friends.* Use the telephone to stay in touch with those who live far away (use a phone discount plan). Contact with loved ones keeps you involved with people and helps to avoid isolation.

6. *Find a physical activity that also engages your mind.* Nature photography, nature walks, gardening, and bird watching all help you to coordinate body and mind.

7. *Be a letter writer.* Writing letters to friends and the local newspapers or keeping a diary all help to keep your mind active.

8. *Be a puzzle solver.* Whether jigsaw puzzles or word games or board games, all puzzles help to keep your mind and vocabulary agile and alive.

9. *Be a joiner.* Join or organize clubs with people with common interests. Meeting and interacting with stimulating people is the spice of life.

10. *Travel with others.* Interesting companions and new sights, sounds, and sensations keep your mind sparkling.

The Second Test
of Adaptability

• • • •

12
....

Test #2

Now that you've gone through most of this book and had an opportunity to take a number of interesting tests, here is another chance to take the Test of Adaptability. The other tests are important, but they are intentionally more narrow in their focus. The adaptability test gives a very wide view of your ability to adapt in a number of areas.

Test #2 is intended for use as a reappraisal of your original self-evaluation or as a check against your original point scores. As we indicated earlier in the book, it's a good idea to get at least two separate readings of your mental health, corresponding to two different moods and circumstances. This second test can also be used to measure how your mental health might possibly change over time. For calculation of your point scores and the interpretations, refer to Chapters 3 and 4.

CHECKLIST OF YOUR EMOTIONAL WELL-BEING

Characteristic #1: Tension

Do you have these typical behaviors and symptoms?

___   1. Your tension has a cause in the present or past. (p. 142)

___   2. You can do something that helps you to relieve your tension. (p. 142)

___   3. You have clear-cut signs of tension (agitation, rapid breathing, sweating). (p. 152)

___   4. Your tension may sometimes inhibit your ability to work. (p. 152)

___   5. You have signs of tension with no apparent cause. (p. 159)

___   6. Your tension inhibits your work most of the time. (p. 159)

___   7. You are often dependent on strong defenses to make your tension bearable. (p. 175)

___   8. You have periods of nearly unbearable anxiety with no obvious cause or understanding. (p. 175)

___   9. Your tension feels unbearable without medication. (p. 186)

___ 10. Your tension is only relieved by disturbed thinking (distortions, hallucinations, grossly inappropriate plans). (p. 186)

Characteristic #2: Mood

Do you have these typical behaviors and symptoms?

___ 1. Your mood swings have a specific cause. (p. 143)

___ 2. You usually have a sense of humor. (p. 143)

___ 3. Your moods can be intense, but they pass within a short time. (p. 143)

___ 4. You are often easily upset, moody, or intolerant of others. (p. 153)

___ 5. You use explosive humor as a tension release. (p. 153)

___ 6. Your moods often last for long periods. (p. 160)

___ 7. You have periodic hysterical behavior. (p. 160)

___ 8. You have strong emotional expressions, often without apparent reason. (p. 160)

___ 9. You often use a hostile sense of humor (sarcasm, etc.). (p. 160)

___ 10. You have mild ongoing fears and phobias. (p. 160)

___ 11. You take unnecessary risks to overcome your fears. (p. 160)

___ 12. You have specific blocked or flattened emotions (e.g., love, hate). (p. 160)

___ 13. Your background moods often affect your ability to work, love, and play. (p. 176)

___ 14. You often have ongoing depressed, unhappy states. (p. 176)

___ 15. You have made suicide attempts, or you have frequent thoughts about suicide. (p. 176)

___ 16. You can get "high" on ideas, but you have problems in following through. (p. 176)

___ 17. You have self-destructive, risk-taking behavior. (p. 176)

___ 18. You often have periods of hysterical behavior (tantrums, emotional outbursts, or destructive behavior). (p. 176)

___ 19. You experience delusions, thought disorders, or hallucinations. (pp. 187–188)

____ 20. You have severe depressions, are often unreachable, or you shut down your work or love involvements. (p. 188)

Characteristic #3: Thought

Do you have these typical behaviors and symptoms?

____ 1. You are able to gather and process information easily. (p. 144)

____ 2. Your thoughts, of whatever kind, do not upset you for long. (p. 144)

____ 3. Your thoughts usually help you to carry out your plans. (p. 144)

____ 4. Your thoughts are intensely, narrowly focused on your task or problem. (p. 153)

____ 5. You experience tension release through your thoughts (e.g., passive, aggressive, or sexual thoughts). (p. 153)

____ 6. You often block out all but important information. (p. 153)

____ 7. You have a tendency to analyze rather than experience your feelings. (p. 163)

____ 8. You often question your ability to feel important emotions. (p. 163)

____ 9. You often experience obsessive worrying or negative self-talk. (p. 163)

____ 10. You often have chronic distortions of reality. (p. 178)

____ 11. You are often alert to an unspecified danger. (p. 178)

____ 12. You often screen out or miss important information. (p. 178)

____ 13. You have repetitive or bothersome thoughts that disrupt your living. (p. 178)

___ 14. Your thoughts often stop you from experiencing strong feelings (e.g., love, anger). (p. 178)

___ 15. You have great difficulty in making decisions. (p. 178)

___ 16. You have continual obsessive thoughts. (p. 190)

___ 17. You have gross perceptual distortions (i.e., visual or auditory hallucinations). (p. 190)

Characteristic #4: Activity

Do you have these typical behaviors and symptoms?

___ 1. You have enthusiasm and interest in doing and participating, and you have a sense of competence. (p. 145)

___ 2. You can take risks and be resilient; you can dare to be mediocre, or even fail and try again. (p. 145)

___ 3. You can handle either continuous ongoing activity or stop-and-start types of activity. (p. 145)

___ 4. According to your temperament, you usually have lots of activity or little activity. (p. 154)

___ 5. You often have anxiety about new risks, or you often feel overloaded. (p. 155)

___ 6. You often use ritualistic words and behavior. (p. 155)

___ 7. You are often hyperactive with no particular purpose or result. (p. 164)

___ 8. You require much inspiration or feedback in order to work adequately. (p. 164)

___ 9. You are usually unable to take risks. (p. 164)

___ 10. You generally avoid new activities. (p. 180)

___ 11. Your coping activities (skills) are no longer able to relieve your tension. (p. 180)

___ 12. You have no pleasure in your accomplishments, your activities are often solitary, and you feel pain if they are not completed. (p. 180)

___ 13. You are frequently engaged in compulsive, ritualistic activities. (p. 191)

___ 14. You have extreme difficulty in changing your patterns of activity. (p. 191)

Characteristic #5: Organization/Control

Do you have these typical behaviors and symptoms?

___ 1. You are able to sit still and address yourself to tasks for the necessary periods of time. (p. 147)

___ 2. You can work in the absence of inspiration or feedback. (p. 147)

___ 3. You can plan and carry out solutions to multi-step problems. (p. 147)

___ 4. You are able to learn from your own experience. (p. 147)

___ 5. You are free to act differently under varying circumstances. (p. 147)

___ 6. Your anxiety often stimulates you to take action. (p. 155)

___ 7. You often find yourself lying or cheating when you are under pressure. (p. 155)

___ 8. You are becoming increasingly rigid: you require clearcut guidelines, or you need perfect conditions in order to function. (p. 166)

___ 9. You regularly feel that you are being overextended. (p. 166)

___ 10. Unpredictable events are often able to disrupt or to negatively influence your performance. (p. 166)

___ 11. You are involved in occasional impulsive behaviors. (p. 166)

___ 12. Your personal rituals often interfere with your work (e.g., sharpening pencils). (p. 166)

___ 13. You have a limited capacity for self-insight and for change. (p. 166)

___ 14. Your behavior is often mechanical. (p. 181)

___ 15. Unexpected minor events often cause you to stop work or to stop activities of love and play. (p. 181)

___ 16. In order to function, you often find yourself performing obsessive rituals. (p. 181)

___ 17. You often display impulsive behavior that disrupts your plans; you don't learn from your mistakes or experience. (p. 181)

___ 18. You have very little self-control; you are easily influenced by outside suggestion or by inner feelings. (p. 192)

___ 19. Your feelings generally make it impossible to work. (p. 192)

___ 20. You are often involved in disturbing, impulsive behavior. (p. 192)

Characteristic #6: Interpersonal Relationships

Do you have these typical behaviors and symptoms?

___ 1. You can be a friend and you can have friends. (p. 148)

___ 2. You have an increasing capacity for intimacy with others. (p. 148)

___ 3. When you withdraw emotionally or become aggressive, it usually has a clear cause, and it soon passes. (p. 148)

____ 4. You use your upset feelings to seek attention from others or to manipulate others. (p. 156)

____ 5. You are often anxious to please others. (p. 156)

____ 6. You are often unwilling or unable to "play." (p. 156)

____ 7. You are often overemotional in your interpersonal relationships. (p. 157)

____ 8. You are often irritable with others. (p. 157)

____ 9. You often find yourself interacting with others in a compulsive or inappropriate manner. (p. 168)

____ 10. You must always get your own way; you are unable to compromise. (p. 168)

____ 11. You can be scapegoated by others, or you can be a bully. (p. 168)

____ 12. You often prematurely initiate one-to-one relationships that you later regret. (p. 168)

____ 13. You have stormy or deteriorating friendships, and you often hold grudges. (p. 168)

____ 14. You generally need constant outside support or approval. (p. 168)

____ 15. You often experience feelings of low self-esteem. (p. 170)

____ 16. You are often somewhat antisocial in your behavior, or you feel alienated. (p. 169)

____ 17. You are extremely dependent on others, or you have a strong need to manipulate others. (p. 182)

____ 18. You often hold extreme grudges against other people. (p. 182)

____ 19. You live in a world of your own, unable to relate to others. (p. 193)

____ 20. You are frequently involved in antisocial behavior (e.g., lying, cheating, stealing, or physical attacks). (p. 193)

Characteristic #7: Physical

Do you have these typical behaviors and symptoms?

___ 1. You have stable patterns of eating, good digestion, healthy skin, and normal breathing, sleeping, and weight. (p. 150)

___ 2. You have relatively quick recovery from an illness or an accident. (p. 150)

___ 3. You have a sense of physical well-being. (p.150)

___ 4. You have many fluctuations in eating and sleeping patterns, or changes in weight, minor gastrointestinal (GI) problems, blemishes. (p. 158)

___ 5. You often feel tense, tired, or exhausted. (p. 158)

___ 6. You intentionally use drugs or alcohol in order to cope. (p. 158)

___ 7. You have periodic skin blemishes, GI problems, obesity, lack of appetite, sleep disturbances, or headaches. (p. 171)

___ 8. You have physical tics and/or stuttering. (p. 171)

___ 9. You have many complaints about your health, often with no clearly defined symptoms. (p. 172)

___ 10. You often use drugs and alcohol or seek medical help to "feel better." (p. 171)

___ 11. You are involved in episodes of drug abuse, often reinforced by your friends or contacts. (p. 171)

___ 12. You appear stiff and/or uptight in your physical mannerisms. (p. 183)

___ 13. You have ongoing psychosomatic problems—ulcers, colitis, insomnia, migraines, absence of menses, anorexia—often without a clear-cut cause. (p. 183)

___ 14. You medicate yourself with drugs or alcohol, often alone, in order to cope. (p. 183)

___ 15. You are continually exhausted, without apparent reason. (p. 183)

___ 16. You display bizarre physical postures. (p. 194)

___ 17. You have many ongoing physical problems, some without apparent cause. (p. 194)

___ 18. You have serious addictions (e.g., drugs and alcohol, sexual behavior, eating disorders, gambling). (p. 195)

Checklist for Characteristic #1: Tension

Refer to the checklists on the preceding pages. Transfer your checks to the boxes on this page by shading the boxes that correspond to your Tension behavior.

Remember, your behavior may fall into several stages of emotional well-being.

NORMAL	STATE OF ALERT	ANXIOUS COPING	ANXIOUS CHARACTER	DISTURBED BEHAVIOR
1. ☐				
2. ☐				
	3. ☐			
	4. ☐			
		5. ☐		
		6. ☐		
			7. ☐	
			8. ☐	
				9. ☐
				10. ☐

Checklist for Characteristic #2: Mood

Shade in the boxes that correspond to your Mood behavior.
Remember, your behavior may fall into several stages of emotional well-being.

NORMAL	STATE OF ALERT	ANXIOUS COPING	ANXIOUS CHARACTER	DISTURBED BEHAVIOR
1. ☐				
2. ☐				
3. ☐				
	4. ☐			
	5. ☐			
		6. ☐		
		7. ☐		
		8. ☐		
		9. ☐		
		10. ☐		
		11. ☐		
		12. ☐		
			13. ☐	
			14. ☐	
			15. ☐	
			16. ☐	
			17. ☐	
			18. ☐	
				19. ☐
				20. ☐

Checklist for Characteristic #3: Thought

Shade in the boxes that correspond to your Thought behavior.
   Remember, your behavior may fall into several stages of emotional well-being.

NORMAL	STATE OF ALERT	ANXIOUS COPING	ANXIOUS CHARACTER	DISTURBED BEHAVIOR
1. ☐				
2. ☐				
3. ☐				
	4. ☐			
	5. ☐			
	6. ☐			
		7. ☐		
		8. ☐		
		9. ☐		
			10. ☐	
			11. ☐	
			12. ☐	
			13. ☐	
			14. ☐	
			15. ☐	
				16. ☐
				17. ☐

Checklist for Characteristic #4: Activity

Shade in the boxes that correspond to your Activity behavior.
Remember, your behavior may fall into several stages of emotional well-being.

NORMAL	STATE OF ALERT	ANXIOUS COPING	ANXIOUS CHARACTER	DISTURBED BEHAVIOR
1. ☐				
2. ☐				
3. ☐				
	4. ☐			
	5. ☐			
	6. ☐			
		7. ☐		
		8. ☐		
		9. ☐		
			10. ☐	
			11. ☐	
			12. ☐	
				13. ☐
				14. ☐

Checklist for Characteristic #5:
Organization/Control

Shade in the boxes that correspond to your Organization/Control behavior.

Remember, your behavior may fall into several stages of emotional well-being.

NORMAL	STATE OF ALERT	ANXIOUS COPING	ANXIOUS CHARACTER	DISTURBED BEHAVIOR
1. ☐				
2. ☐				
3. ☐				
4. ☐				
5. ☐				
	6. ☐			
	7. ☐			
		8. ☐		
		9. ☐		
		10. ☐		
		11. ☐		
		12. ☐		
		13. ☐		
			14. ☐	
			15. ☐	
			16. ☐	
			17. ☐	
				18. ☐
				19. ☐
				20. ☐

Checklist for Characteristic #6:
Interpersonal Relationships

Shade in the boxes that correspond to your Interpersonal Relationships behavior.

Remember, your behavior may fall into several stages of emotional well-being.

NORMAL	STATE OF ALERT	ANXIOUS COPING	ANXIOUS CHARACTER	DISTURBED BEHAVIOR
1. ☐				
2. ☐				
3. ☐				
	4. ☐			
	5. ☐			
	6. ☐			
	7. ☐			
	8. ☐			
		9. ☐		
		10. ☐		
		11. ☐		
		12. ☐		
		13. ☐		
		14. ☐		
		15. ☐		
		16. ☐		
			17. ☐	
			18. ☐	
				19. ☐
				20. ☐

Checklist for Characteristic #7: Physical

Shade in the boxes that correspond to your Physical behavior.
Remember, your behavior may fall into several stages of emotional well-being.

NORMAL	STATE OF ALERT	ANXIOUS COPING	ANXIOUS CHARACTER	DISTURBED BEHAVIOR
1. ☐				
2. ☐				
3. ☐				
	4. ☐			
	5. ☐			
	6. ☐			
		7. ☐		
		8. ☐		
		9. ☐		
		10. ☐		
		11. ☐		
			12. ☐	
			13. ☐	
			14. ☐	
			15. ☐	
				16. ☐
				17. ☐
				18. ☐

EMOTIONAL WELL-BEING BAR GRAPH

If you have forgotten the method for computing point scores, refer to the explanation on page 35. Once you have computed total scores for each of the seven characteristics, shade in the second Emotional Well-Being Bar Graph. Compare this graph of your mental condition with the one you drew on page 55. If the two graphs differ greatly, it is an indication that your mental health may have changed over time.

The knowledge you have gained in studying this self-evaluation guide may be therapeutic. Introspection, or the ability to look within, is the base upon which psychology has developed. We hope this book has helped you to learn about yourself and to become more aware of your tensions, your strengths, and your behavior patterns in everyday life. Knowledge is power. Congratulations on finishing the Second Test of Adaptability.

Mental Health Bar Graph

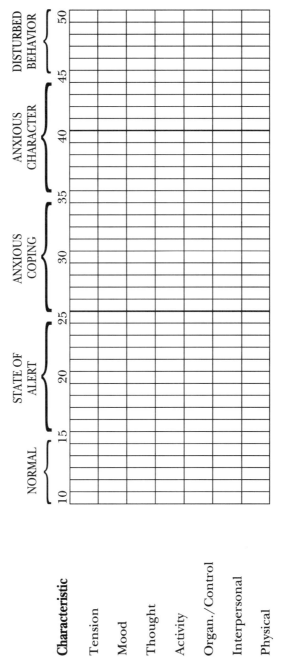

POINTS

Characteristic	NORMAL	STATE OF ALERT	ANXIOUS COPING	ANXIOUS CHARACTER	DISTURBED BEHAVIOR
	10 15	20 25	30 35	40 45	50
Tension					
Mood					
Thought					
Activity					
Organ./Control					
Interpersonal					
Physical					

10–25 Within realm of expected behavior. Normal functioning. May want help with specific problems. Preventive therapy.

26–40 Serious stresses and problems. Professional help may be advisable. Functioning with difficulty.

40–50 Marginal functioning. Seek professional help.

There Is Help

····

13
....

How Do I Know
I Need Help?[9]

Although not complete, the following list contains 14 definite warning signs that may indicate that you need help. Please review this checklist. *Signs of distress are not always obvious.*

Some distress signals to look for:

____ 1. Persistent feelings of dissatisfaction.

____ 2. Problems with your child's behavior, school adjustment, or performance.

____ 3. Sexual problems or concerns.

____ 4. Unexplainable fatigue or difficulty in sleeping.

____ 5. Difficulties in talking with your fiancé, spouse, children, parents, family members, friends, or co-workers.

____ 6. Feelings of loneliness, moodiness, depression, sadness, failure, stress, or anxiety.

____ 7. The need for tranquilizers, energizers, or sleeping aids.

____ 8. Family stress caused by chronic illnesses *or* illness in which stress plays a major role.

____ 9. Problems with alcohol or drugs.

___ 10. Frequent financial difficulties.

___ 11. Difficulty in setting or reaching goals.

___ 12. Drastic weight fluctuations or irregular eating patterns.

___ 13. Work difficulties, frequent job changes, problems with co-workers.

___ 14. Difficulties with anger, hostility, or violence.

If you have some of these signs on a regular basis, you need help.

What to Expect When You Go for Help[10]

If you or a friend decides that you need help, it's important to know where to go and what to expect. If you call a hotline, you'll probably reach a trained volunteer or worker, not a professional counselor. That person may help you to sort through a current problem or crisis. His or her main job, however, is to give you information or to refer you to the right resources. For instance, if you had a drug problem you might get a referral to a drug treatment program or a local clinic. If it were an emergency, you would get an immediate referral to a hospital emergency room.

CHOOSING A MENTAL HEALTH PROFESSIONAL

If you're looking for a mental health professional, it's a very different pursuit. Before you make a call, you need to consider these questions: Do you need someone with special expertise? Do you need a mental health professional who specializes in working with adolescents, or older people, or people with sexual problems or substance abuse problems? Do you prefer a therapist located near you or in a particular area? How much will you be able to pay for therapy? Will your insurance cover the types of services you need? (Will you be reimbursed?)

If you go to a community mental health agency (or a social/family service agency), you may pay reduced fees based on your income, but you may not always have a choice of therapists. And, you may not be able to talk with the therapist before the first session.

If you decide to go for private therapy, it may be useful to select two or three professionals who you think may be able to help you. You can then call each of them and conduct a short interview. (For a list of possible referral sources, see Appendix C.)

Conducting a Phone Interview

Introduce yourself and explain that you are considering therapy. Ask them if they have time to answer a few questions. If they don't, find a time convenient for both of you for a phone meeting. During the phone interview, you might ask the following: What are their qualifications and experience or training? What kind of license do they have? What is their fee? (If it is not affordable, ask them if there is a "sliding scale fee.") Is there a charge for an initial consultation? Is insurance accepted? What type of therapy is used for your type of problem? Does the therapist have experience in treating your type of problem? Ask for an explanation of any new terms. What hours are available for an appointment?

A telephone interview will help you select the therapist you think you could work with. After speaking with these therapists, reflect on how you felt about each of them. Were they easy to talk to? Did they seem supportive? Did they answer your questions clearly? And were you comfortable speaking to them? Trust your instincts—you're picking someone whom you will be speaking to about very personal and confidential matters.

THE FIRST SESSION

During the first session you will want the following information: How long are the therapy sessions? How often will appointments be scheduled? What happens if you're late or miss an appointment? How can you reach your therapist in an emergency? How will insurance billings or payments be handled? When do you pay for sessions? Will anyone see your records and will the sessions be kept confidential? What kind of treatment approaches will be taken, and how long does the therapist anticipate you'll be in therapy? Will he or she be available for phone calls between sessions? These are the kinds of questions people ask in a first session.

If you do not feel comfortable after the first few sessions, you need to seriously consider getting a new therapist, or you should discuss any reservations you have before you continue. You will be investing your time, money, energy, and trust in this person, so it's important that you make a good decision.

THE BEGINNING OF THERAPY

At the beginning of therapy, you and the therapist will talk about what you want to accomplish and you will discuss treatment approaches. The role of the therapist is to help you express yourself and to help you to define and resolve your problems. Therapy can be painful, especially at the beginning when things often get worse before they get better. Over time, however, therapy should be a rewarding experience that helps you to deal more effectively with your problems, and to gain self-understanding and self-acceptance. Ideally psychotherapy can be a voyage of self-discovery.

LICENSED MENTAL
HEALTH PROFESSIONALS

Here is a list to help you become familiar with the different types of mental health providers.

- A Licensed Clinical Social Worker (LSCW, or CSW) has completed a master's degree in social work, with additional post-graduate work practicing under the supervision of a licensed therapist. Social Workers may provide psychotherapy, rehabilitation, and case management services in hospitals, clinics, and in private practice.

- A Marriage, Family, Child Counselor (MFCC), must complete at least a master's degree in marriage and family therapy. He or she specializes in counseling families, adolescents, and children.

- A Psychiatrist is a medical doctor (M.D.) with special education and training in psychiatry. He or she can diagnose and treat the biological causes of mental disorders and prescribe medications and other therapies.

- A Psychologist must complete a Ph.D. in psychology. He or she can evaluate, diagnose, and treat nervous, emotional, and mental disorders as well as problems of everyday life and the psychological aspects of injury and disease. Most psychologists have specialized expertise in testing, psychological evaluation, and psychotherapy.

- Other mental health professionals you may encounter include psychiatric nurses, social workers, substance abuse counselors, psychiatric technicians, case managers, and specialized therapists. Some of these specialties require licenses.

Appendix A

Introduction to the Theory of the Five Stages of Mental Health

WELCOME TO PSYCH 101

This section of the book will give you a complete overview of the five stages of mental health. In a sense, it is a complete course in basic human psychology. If you have studied psychology, this section will be a refresher and a breeze. If you have never studied psychology, you may need to read some of the sections more than once in order to fully understand all of the principles presented. In either case, we hope the section will serve as a valuable reference for you as you continue to explore your own state of emotional well-being.

THE THEORY OF THE FIVE STAGES OF MENTAL HEALTH

The idea of looking at mental health in terms of stages has gained much acceptance, both in research and clinical psychology. There is some degree of arbitrariness in designating categories, but that is only natural since human nature is by definition not capable of being captured live, like a butterfly in a net. So we are always dealing in descriptions of reality that can never perfectly describe reality itself.

Furthermore, in an area of such delicacy and popular misconception as mental illness, one must be careful to point out that all categories, including the ones in this book, are relative. There is no such thing as "a normal person," "an anxious person," or "a disturbed person," who fits exactly into any medical or psychological model. These labels reflect working hypotheses. At best, they are generalizations and abstractions that psychologists have been able to develop. Why? Because, they enable mental health professionals to classify people and to make better use of available medical resources. Nevertheless, please realize they are labels and nothing more.

In fact, these labels are powerful and should not be used casually. In American society, calling someone *neurotic, unbalanced,* or *mentally ill* can be a severe injury, far more harmful to individual well-being than the symptoms upon which this diagnosis is based. So, let's be careful and approach our exploration with a sense of proportion, and a sense of humor.

The objective is not to determine whether you are "crazy," but to determine the degree to which the stresses and problems in your life reduce your adaptability. Everyone has problems. Everyone has defenses. Everyone engages in behavior that, from a clinical perspective, could be called abnormal. The checklists in this book that you have completed enable you to judge to what extent your behavior reflects a particular level of adaptability. More specifically, they tell you in what areas your behavior reflects stress and what kinds of activities and symptoms are worth your concern and possible modification.

What the Categories Really Mean

Please remember, there is no hierarchy of human worth or perfection. If you are a stage three personality (anxious coping) rather than stage one (normal adaptability), this does not mean that you are inferior or less aware. It is simply an indication that the stresses in your life are affecting your behavior to a larger degree than normal or desirable for a happy, balanced life. This may be a reflection of your current social circumstances, a difficult family situation, a difficult childhood, a stressful job, financial problems, a loss of religious or spiritual faith, or more likely a combination of all these and other experiences in your life.

Your Mental Health Changes Over Time

All of these factors are capable of changing, and no person is immune to stress. *Your mental health changes throughout time just as your physical health does.* There is little evidence suggesting the existence of so-called permanently defective personalities. *Your state of emotional well-being is a reflection of your personality traits and your immediate life situation.* Both factors are subject to change.

Considering all of the "slings and arrows of outrageous fortune" to which human beings are vulnerable, as Shakespeare would say, it is perhaps no small wonder that the great majority of men and women manage to maintain, more or less, a lifelong pattern of functional mental health!

In both the discussion and definition of the stages of mental health that follow, the terms *normal, abnormal, anxious,* and *disturbed* will be used as if they were true scientific labels; in fact, they are only descriptive terms. It is merely a fiction, but a useful one. Only in this way can an accurate picture be drawn of your mental health.

STAGE ONE: NORMAL ADAPTABILITY

How shall we define normal behavior? Is anyone really normal? From a scientific point of view, there is no such thing. *The idea of normalcy is so influenced by cultural values that an objective cross-cultural or universal definition is truly impossible to draw.* But it is fair to say that most Americans do value the goals of democracy, self-determination, material comfort, and achievement. Normalcy is the ability to get along with others and to work to achieve these goals, while at the same time finding enjoyment and fulfillment in the privileges and responsibilities that our culture encourages.

Normal Adaptability in an Era of Dramatic Change

We have chosen the idea of normal adaptability for our definition of normalcy. This is as close to a universal definition as any that has been devised. It seems appropriate for our American society, as we come to the end of the twentieth century that we choose a definition that will embrace our ability to adapt to the colossal and rapid changes brought about by technological, economic, social, and psychological factors.

Never before in the history of the world have so many significant changes come about at so fast and so furious a pace. These changes occur at all levels of society—the family (separations, divorces, and remarriages), politics (post–Cold War tensions and major realignments), economics (new insecurities and new opportunities), communications (through global networks the world is literally shrinking), and medicine (people live longer and with greater dependence on external devices than ever before).

The ability to adapt to these changes has become a virtual necessity; regardless of one's individual feelings or opinions or philosophy, change has become an undeniable daily fact of life. We must all adapt our lifestyles in such a manner as to make use of, or to protect ourselves, from the effects of these changes. On an individual level, this amounts to the ability to maintain a sense of meaning and purpose in one's daily life. *A normal person is able to make decisions and not merely to react. He or she is able to accept the turns of fortune with, if not equanimity, at least a sense of balance. His or her life, is for the most part, an integrated whole. A failure in one area does not devalue his or her entire identity.*

This requires that there be balance in work, love, and play— the ideal of Aristotle. Individuals who are committed in equal measure to all three areas of human life are less subject to disintegration than those who place all their emotional and physical energies in a single area. Life is full of changes. People who place their entire self in the area of work, neglecting love (family) and play (sports, hobbies, socializing, friendships), decrease their overall adaptability. If they define their existence in terms of achievement in their work, they will find that if for external reasons (poor health, old age, economic recession) or boredom (loss of interest, disillusionment with the larger purpose of their work, loss of faith in their employer) their work loses meaning, then so will their life. They will become demoralized, confused, and unable to function. The same is true in the areas of love and play. A person who defines existence in terms of a single love relationship will become demoralized if this relationship is destroyed. The connection between unrequited love, broken love relationships, and emotional despair is testimony to the danger of overinvesting in a single individual all of your emotional energies. In these cases, when there is a loss, there is nothing to take the place of the lost object or activity.

For this reason, the notion of balance is at the core of the definition of normalcy. Only with balanced interests can an individual guard against the stress that loss, or the threat of loss, in a significant area produces. Losses must constantly be confronted in all human relationships and activities. This is the one constant in human experience; the inevitability of change and loss. Only by participating fully in all three areas of life— work, love, and play—is it possible to diminish the devastating effects of loss in any single area. Balanced participation in the three areas of life permits the experience of many losses that, in terms of the individual as a whole, are small "partial" deaths; that is, they are less devastating than that of a single total loss so invested with meaning, as to equal the death of the individual personality *in total.*

In essence, normal adaptability implies the ability to function in everyday life. There may be inner conflicts but they do not impede your ability to act, to grow, and to change. Your adaptation to your job, your family, and your social and cultural situation are relatively conflict free. You do not question the basic facts of your existence, but have a solid feeling of who you are, what you do, and why you do it. In the psychologist's terms you have a strong sense of identity. You may not like certain parts of your personality, but you do not have difficulty defining yourself. Basically, you accept yourself as you are. You do not suffer from an identity crisis.

Checklist for Normal Adaptability

The following checklist covers the seven categories of behavior characteristics outlined in Chapter 2. Refer to these definitions before reading this section. Here are listed examples of behavior for each characteristic that can be considered "normal." Of course, this list does not exhaust the possibilities of normal behavior. *If you wish, you might read through the checklist once briefly and then read it a second time, making light pencil marks next to those items which apply to your own behavior.*

1. TENSION

Your Typical Behavior
- Your tension has cause in the present or the past.
- You can "do" something that helps to relieve tension when it arises.

Explanation and Examples

You do not experience tension or nervousness randomly. You do not find yourself tense or nervous for no apparent reason. You usually become nervous under pressure. Whether this pressure is caused by a visit from your mother-in-law, the preparation for an important dinner party, or a public address that you must give, is not significant.

Each person faces acts or activities that create tension either in anticipation or performance. This is normal, particularly when there are concrete actions you can perform to reduce these tensions. These actions may consist of nothing more than discussing the anticipated visit from an in-law with a spouse and airing your worries, practicing your speech in front of friends beforehand, or checking to be sure that you have all the ingredients at hand for a success-ful dinner party.

It is not important what causes your tension, as long as you know what it is. Equally, what you do to reduce tension is not so important as long as it works (as long as it does not create sig-nificant problems, as may be the case with the uncontrolled use of drugs or alcohol).

2. MOOD

Your Typical Behavior
- Changes in your moods have causes.
- You have a sense of humor even when you experience intense moods.
- Your moods can be intense, but they pass within a short time.

Explanation and Examples

Changes in mood usually have causes. A cause may be righteous indignation over a lie or an unfair business practice perpet-uated against you, producing a mood of intense anger. A ro-mantic movie in which the heroine dies may provoke a mood of sadness. What your mood is and what causes it is not as important as your ability to identify and gauge your reaction to specific events in everyday life.

Even when feeling angry or depressed you can still re-tain a sense of humor. A sense of humor is the ability to step back from yourself and your problems and enjoy either the humorous aspects of your own situation or that of others. The presence of a sense of humor includes the ability to enjoy the company of others and to be entertained. In short, it is the ability to laugh. *When your anger or melancholy is so in-tense that you are unable to react to the whimsical or lighthearted, it is a sign of overvaluing a particular event or aspect of your life, of losing your mental balance.*

The intensity of a mood, even if the cause is appropriate, may be great. This is normal. *What to look at is the duration of a mood.* Do you find yourself staying angry for hours or days? When you're depressed, does it pass; do you respond to happier situations, or does the mood remain with you for days or even weeks?

3. THOUGHT

Your Typical Behavior
- You are able to secure and process information easily.
- Your thoughts, of whatever kind, do not upset you for long.
- Your thoughts help you to carry out your plans.

Explanation and Examples

Normal thought behavior is where you have some control over your thoughts and where your thoughts help you to act. In our culture "appropriate thinking" is normal thinking. The ability to define a problem and think about the different kinds of information and different ways of organizing information toward a solution is characteristic of appropriate thinking.

Normal thinking is more than just problem-solving ability. Under thought behavior are included fantasies, daydreams, and general contemplation. Sometimes fantasies and daydreams can be erotic (as with sexual fantasies), or exhilarating (sports fantasies), or frightening (highway commuter fantasies). Often they are disruptive and difficult to integrate with everyday life. The characteristic of normal thought is not the exclusion of such thoughts, but the ability to control them. Roughly, it could be called the ability to control your thought, or to "snap out of it" when your mind wanders off into your own private world.

Normal thought behavior is that which is free of obsessive thoughts that interfere with the processing of information. It is the ability to relate to the external world in an active way. It is the ability to make decisions once you have processed information and to act on information you have thought about. It is freedom from circular thinking and thinking that does not contribute toward solving problems, providing satisfaction, or reducing anxiety. This might include negative self-talk, which refers to inner self-judgments and thoughts that are negative.

4. ACTIVITY

Your Typical Behavior
- You have enthusiasm and interest in doing and participating—individually or in groups—in work or play, which brings you a sense of competence.
- You can take risks and be resilient; you can dare to be mediocre, or even fail and try again.
- You can handle either continuous activity, or stop-and-start types of activity.

Explanation and Examples

Normal activity implies more than just going through the motions. Whether the activity is working, recreation, socializing, or lovemaking, it should bring a positive sense of self-fulfillment. Activity that brings a sense of competence also brings a sense of well-being. It helps you to establish your sense of identity and is a sign that you have a place in the world that is appreciated and valued by others.

Mentally adaptable people are not afraid to engage in new kinds of activities. They do not shun new experiences and new opportunities for growth. They are not afraid to take risks. They do not need constant success. They do not need to limit themselves to those activities and those relationships in which they know in advance that they will succeed or be warmly accepted. They are not afraid of being just average Joes or Janes. They are not afraid of being less than the best at everything. They are not perfectionists and are willing to participate in areas of personal weakness as well as strength.

For example, is a successful businessman willing to be a mediocre tennis player, or does he insist on playing only if he can achieve a high level of skill? Is an honors student willing to get on a dance floor and look a little foolish in front of her friends because she's not a very good dancer? Are you frightened of learning to play the guitar or of singing in a group because you're afraid you won't be any good?

When you reject possible activities even before trying them out because you're afraid of failing, your activity is not normal. (This, of course, varies for older people and for those with physical disabilities for whom risk-taking and engaging in new activities may be inappropriate. Even for these groups, however, within a range of safety, there should be a willingness to try new activities and make new friends.)

Even more important than risk-taking as a measure of good mental health is the notion of resilience. *Resilience is your ability to recover from setbacks or failures.* Most men and women who are successful in life are those who are able to recover after a disappointment and either try again or learn from their failures. Resilience, both mental and physical, decreases over time—you do not recover from injuries as rapidly as you used to. Failures become more difficult to accept in key areas of life, such as marriage and work. Nonetheless, as long as you survive you maintain a degree of resiliency, and in most cases, more than you give yourself credit for.

Normal behavior is measured by your ability to engage in either uneven or continuous activities. Uneven activities are those which stop and start, and require haphazard participation. Many games are of this nature. They require the ability to make sudden bursts of energy in specific areas. Continuous activities are those such as bookkeeping or driving, which require constant attention over long periods of time. Each type of activity requires different qualities and the ability to engage in both types indicates a reserve of mental energies and general adaptability.

5. ORGANIZATION/CONTROL

Your Typical Behavior
- You are able to sit still and address yourself to a task for the required period of time.
- You can work in the absence of inspiration or feedback.
- You can plan and carry out solutions to multi-step problems.
- You can learn from your own experience.
- You are free to act differently under varying circumstances.

Explanation and Examples

Normal organization/control behavior has certain attributes in common with normal activity behavior. How are your activities organized? Do you have patience and endurance for tedious tasks? Can you work alone without encouragement or rewards from others? Can you work well even when you're not in the mood to work? Can you carry out long-term projects that require careful preparation and planning? Do you learn from your failures and apply this knowledge to future projects? Are you able to call upon different kinds of behavioral skills in solving problems and to shift approaches smoothly and flexibly when necessary? If you answer "yes" to all of these questions you are clearly an adaptable and healthy individual.

An example of the freedom to act differently under varying circumstances is the ability to complete a project that requires different kinds of skills. A filmmaker who can sell his idea for making a film to investors, organize a film crew, and participate in the filming and meticulous editing process demonstrates a variety of behavioral skills, from interpersonal (selling the idea and organizing a crew), to concentration (editing), to intuitive and uneven activity (the actual filming). The work of a diplomat or a fund-raiser whose projects require the working out of long-term goals, dealing with a variety of different individuals and with unexpected events would also call upon a flexible repertoire of behavioral skills.

Again, as in all the characteristics discussed thus far, *the appropriate behavior for the emotionally healthy person is that which demonstrates the highest level of adaptability to the external world.*

6. INTERPERSONAL RELATIONSHIPS

Your Typical Behavior

- Your interpersonal skills have developed over time.
- You can be a friend, and you can have friends.
- You have an increasing capacity for intimacy with others.
- When you withdraw emotionally, or become aggressive, it usually has a clear cause, and it soon passes.

Explanation and Examples

Normal interpersonal behavior is that in which you have a range of different kinds of relationships that call forth different degrees of feeling and different attitudes. You are able to be dependent on others, and to allow others to be dependent on you.

Of the many psychological theories that describe stages of personality development, we will use the one authored by psychiatrist, Harry Stack Sullivan (1892–1949). *Sullivan developed a theory of personality and interpersonal relations in which each stage of development—infancy, childhood, juvenile, preadolescence, early and later adolescence, and mature adulthood—was associated with distinct types of interpersonal skills.*

For instance, the juvenile era (ages 5 to 9) is associated with the abilities to compete, cooperate, and compromise with others, but not with the ability to establish intimacy, which is an interpersonal skill achieved only in maturity. *Sullivan argued that the process of personality development was cumulative. You could not demonstrate the higher interpersonal skills until you had passed through the lower stages.* Sullivan cited many cases of "chronically juvenile" people who are chronologically adults. By this he meant that certain individuals never fully develop their interpersonal skills.

Although we do not fully accept Sullivan's theory of stages, it is useful to think of approximate stages of growth and appropriate behavior corresponding to different and changing age levels. When an adult engages in childish behavior, is excessively competitive, or is unable to establish intimacy, his behavior becomes a problem for himself and for others, and is a sign of poor emotional development and lack of healthy interpersonal behavior.

The capacity for intimacy is the ability to associate closely with another person. You are able to make yourself vulnerable to another and share your most intimate thoughts and feelings. You are also able to accept the vulnerability of another without anxiety or destructive results. You give of yourself from within; from who you really are, and not from the image that you try to project to the world at large.

The capacity for intimacy varies among different individuals, but all persons have needs for dealing with suffering and personal despair that can only be satisfied by intimate relationships with others. In general, the greater the intimacy you achieve, the more productive your relationship will be with regard to your mental balance and behavior in other areas. The capacity for intimacy is not exactly identical with the capacity to love, which may or may not be accompanied by intimacy.

It is normal to withdraw from another or even attack another when you are mistreated, insulted, humiliated, exploited, or otherwise have your trust abused. When you find yourself exploding against another, fighting, or feeling uncomfortable, it is important to know why this happens. *When such antisocial behavior occurs without provocation, or is resorted to before any attempt at communicating with another is made, this would be a case of abnormal interpersonal behavior.* Often a person will explode at another (especially a spouse or member of the immediate family) without knowing exactly why. To a certain extent this is normal, as many subtle messages are conveyed by persons who live together in close contact, which are often of an aggressive nature without being obvious. The repeated occurrence of such events, however, is not normal.

7. PHYSICAL

Your Typical Behavior
- You have a stable gastrointestinal system.
- You have stable skin and weight conditions.
- You have regular sleeping and breathing patterns.
- You recover rapidly from an illness or an accident.
- You have a sense of feeling well.

Explanation and Examples

Your physical health and your mental health are closely associated. Recent research is finding that many emotional problems correspond to physical ailments, and that there is a close relationship between chemical and biological processes and mental behavior. *Apparently, your physical condition is both a cause and a mirror of your mental condition.*

Gastrointestinal problems are often signs of emotional stress. This is, of course, not always the case. One good indicator of stable mental condition is a stable gastrointestinal system—regularity of bowel movements, comfortable digestion without excessive gas, and freedom from gastrointestinal problems such as heartburn, indigestion, nausea, diarrhea, constipation, and associated stomach and intestinal illnesses.

One of the causes of acne and sudden weight losses and gains is emotional stress. The absence of major acne, and a stable weight condition are signs of mental health. The same is true of breathing and sleeping patterns. Although sleeping and breathing problems are not always the result of mental problems, *the absence of insomnia, asthma, and rapid breathing are signs of positive mental health.*

The rapid recovery from an accident or an illness is also a sign of emotional well-being. Your mental condition often effects your rate of recovery from physical problems, and rapid and complete recovery is a positive sign. (Note that lengthy recovery is not necessarily a sign of mental illness, as physical causes may predominate over mental factors in many cases.) Likewise, *a general sense of feeling well or of physical well-being is an important indicator of normal mental health.*

STAGE TWO: THE STATE OF ALERT

In the above discussion of stage one behavior, normal adaptability has often been used as if it referred to ideal adaptability, which is sought by all but obtained by few. To a certain extent this is true. *No one is completely adaptable. There is no such thing as a perfectly normal person. We all have idiosyncrasies and problems.* It is possible to deviate from the behavior suggested as normal and still be included in the general category of normal. This is the case of behavior that falls into stage two, the state of alert. Again, no one is expected to exhibit precisely these behavior symptoms.

Nonetheless, all of the following behavior patterns are indicators of minor abnormality. They describe the behavior of someone who is stressed or who is under extreme pressure. People are often under extreme pressure in our modern society, and some people hold jobs that are virtually constant emergency situations (e.g., police, firefighters). For people in such situations the following behavior patterns might indeed be normal and appropriate. The question in such a case would be to determine if your responsibilities are too great and if perhaps you would be happier in a less pressured job or life-situation. Behavior problems in this stage often take care of themselves when external pressures are removed, and are not indicators of serious mental stress.

In general, the following conditions are "normal" adjustments to abnormal stress and strain. Such abnormal stresses might be school exams, deadline pressures at work, the breakup or loss of an important interpersonal relationship with spouse, lover, parent, or child, and clear-cut external events such as an economic loss, tragic world events, and deaths of persons upon whom you depend. Under such circumstances you can expect your usual resiliency and adaptability to be impaired. *The purpose of the behavior patterns that follow (a psychologist would call them "defenses") is to relieve tension while permitting effective functioning.* What is lost is general joy and adventure in living. You are forced to just get by, and you cannot really fulfill yourself. You cannot develop or enjoy your entire personality. Nor can you appreciate and constructively enjoy opportunities that you might have, were you behaving in accordance with stage one patterns.

Checklist for the State of Alert Behavior

1. TENSION

Your Typical Behavior
- You have clear-cut signs of tension (agitation, sweating, irregular breathing).
- Your tension has a cause (i.e., exams, disrupted personal relations, a pending operation).
- Your tension may sometimes inhibit work.

Explanation and Examples

In stage two it is not as easy to reduce tension as in stage one. Signs of tension are much clearer and occur more frequently. Your nervousness is, however, still in response to immediate and understandable causes. You do not start sweating spontaneously or become agitated for no apparent reason. You show signs of stress, but only in response to real stresses in your environment—loss of a job, the need for surgery, a divorce, and so forth. *Despite your tension, you will probably still be able to carry out your normal responsibilities.* At times you may find normal work more burdensome and use your tension "symptoms" to avoid normal activities. Your precise reactions will vary according to other factors, such as mood and physical well-being, but you are not at the point at which your tension prohibits you from engaging in work, and carrying out normal responsibilities.

2. MOOD

Your Typical Behavior

- You are easily upset or often moody or intolerant of others.
- You use explosive humor as a tension release.

Explanation and Examples

In stage two, your moods change frequently and are more intense. You are less stable and small problems and disappointments can make you suddenly agitated or depressed. You don't have your normal bounce and enthusiasm. When contradicted you become upset. You do not appreciate surprises or the unexpected as much as you normally would, and you can become intolerant of anyone who does not pay extra attention to your particular mood (happy or sad).

A common symptom in stage two is to become uncustomarily demonstrative of your emotions; to explode with laughter as a means of releasing your built-up tension, or to suddenly start crying, or to explode with angry shouting. You will still be responding to actual situations—a funny joke, a tragic book or movie, poor or inefficient service, inadequate attention. The difference will be in the intensity of your response and the need to release tension in socially acceptable ways; ways upon which you did not previously rely.

3. THOUGHT

Your Typical Behavior

- Your thoughts are intensely, narrowly, and continuously focused on your task or problem.

- You experience tension release through your thoughts (e.g., passive, aggressive, or sexual thoughts).
- You selectively tune out distractions.

Explanation and Examples

In stage two you must struggle with your thoughts in order to act effectively. You do not experience free-flowing, constructive thinking. Problem-solving is not effortless but demands concentrated thinking that is intense and immediate. You cannot allow thoughts to wander, for fear of not being able to return to the problem at hand. You can only think about one problem or a single stage of a problem at a time. *Your thoughts are reactions to situations and not creative solutions.*

The reason you must focus on narrow issues is that you are trying to release tension through thoughts. You imagine acts of aggression against your enemies, or have sexual fantasies or daydreams in which all your problems are solved without any effort on your part. Such fantasies are normal, but in stage two they occur more frequently and serve to distract you from solving your problems in real life. Rather than facilitating action as in stage one, your thoughts prevent and inhibit effective action. You still function and get the job done, but it's more of a struggle.

In stage two you might also find yourself ignoring situations or people that upset you. You will turn yourself off rather than risk potential frustration at hearing things or seeing things you'd rather not think about. *Your inattention is selective, however. You do not ignore really important information and are still able to make important decisions and to process difficult information.*

4. ACTIVITY

Your Typical Behavior
- According to your temperament, you generate lots of activity or little.

- You have anxiety about taking new risks, or you often feel overloaded.
- You often use ritualistic words or behavior.

Explanation and Examples

In stage two your activity level is no longer smooth and stable. You may find yourself cutting down on your activities or scurrying about hurriedly, taking on far more than is possible for the time at your disposal. According to temperament, you are less likely to involve yourself with new activities and are cautious about overextending yourself. You are very much aware of what activites you engage in and are more anxious about how well you will do than in stage one.

Because you have less confidence in your abilities and are more concerned with how your activities demonstrate to others your general state of being and your worth, in stage two you are more likely to seek tricks and gimmicks that will ensure success. To a certain extent, *this use of ritualistic behavior is normal.* By always repeating certain speeches or certain acts you assure yourself a sense of continuity. Such ritualistic behavior is common among athletes who may always play the same song before a contest or wear the same pair of socks while on a hitting streak.

In stage two you are far more dependent on following a set routine in order to ensure success. You are not able to shift as easily from one type of activity to another. You still enjoy your activities but your motivation is as much the anxiety you feel if you don't keep busy, as the positive pleasure of action itself.

5. ORGANIZATION/CONTROL

Your Typical Behavior
- Your anxiety often stimulates you to take action.
- You can lie or cheat under pressure.

Explanation and Examples

In stage two your anxiety directs your action. Your organization is less creative, and you will use any means possible to assure a positive outcome. You may need to play with "a loaded deck," to be sure that nothing unexpected will occur to complicate your plans. *You may still be able to engage in complicated problem-solving and long-term planning, but your tolerance of ambiguity or uncertainty is low.*

An historic example of state of alert behavior is that carried out by former President Richard Nixon's campaigners in 1972, which resulted in the Watergate scandal. Nixon and his associates felt themselves under such extreme pressure to win the election that they were willing to rationalize unethical procedures, as justified in light of the importance (they maintained and tried to make themselves believe) of a Nixon victory to national security.

Had a true emergency existed, their behavior might have been justifiable as normal emergency behavior. Given the actual realities, it was a sign of a more general breakdown.

In stage two the results of your organization and control may be identical to those achieved under normal mental health. The difference is the quality of your planning. You are less likely to come up with elegant or creative solutions and more likely to rely on drudgery and anxiety-directed doggedness to get the job done. *The key is your work is just as effective, but you enjoy it less.*

6. INTERPERSONAL RELATIONSHIPS

Your Typical Behavior

- You use your upset feelings to manipulate others, or to seek attention.
- You have anxiety about pleasing others, or gaining their approval.
- You have an unwillingness or an inability to "play."

- You are often over-emotional in interpersonal relationships.
- You are often irritable with others.

Explanation and Examples

When under emergency stress, interpersonal behavior is the factor that usually deteriorates most. You begin to see yourself as a special person entitled to special consideration. When you're upset, you may use your depression or anger as a means of forcing friends or family to take notice of your problems and to give you special attention and understanding. In stage two you may often be irritable, ready to fly off the handle at the least provocation.

You are less willing to tolerate horseplay or any activity that pokes fun at you or the things you value. *Your ability to compromise or cooperate with others may be reduced and it is harder to achieve intimacy than in stage one.* You take yourself and others much more seriously than necessary and do not have your normal good humor and pleasant disposition.

You may also be anxious to please others and gain their approval. You overreact to criticism and negative feedback. You exaggerate mild disapproval and create friction between yourself and others without intending to. You also become overemotional, showing disproportionate concern or affection for people you aren't really close to. You may react less to people as they really are and more as you pretend they are in some ideal world that exists in your mind more than in the everyday world. As a result, you are less able to appreciate the real strengths and weaknesses of your friends, and you have more difficulty in establishing a wide range of appropriate relationships of different intensities.

In stage two, however, you still have many friends and are able to appreciate their individual qualities, especially in moments of calm or when the stress of your emergency lifestyle or job has passed. You are still pretty much in control of your interpersonal relationships.

7. PHYSICAL

Your Typical Behavior
- You have frequent fluctuations in eating and sleeping patterns, or changes in weight.
- You have minor gastrointestinal problems, and skin blemishes.
- You have a physical sense of tension or tiredness, or of using up your physical reserves.
- You intentionally use drugs or alcohol to cope.

Explanation and Examples

In stage two you may find yourself overeating (or undereating), having difficulty getting to sleep, or suffering from stomach problems such as gas and indigestion. If you are an adolescent or young adult you may be plagued by acne and skin blemishes. You may even have an outbreak of hives or a skin rash.

Physically you don't feel 100 percent. You have a feeling of being pushed to the limits of your endurance, of not having your normal "get up and go." You become tired easily and your muscles are often stiff. You are more accident-prone than normal and when ill, you recover more slowly.

To deal with these problems, you may find yourself taking nonprescription sleeping pills, mild tranquilizers, or stimulants (both legal drugs and illegal drugs, ranging from aspirin to marijuana to amphetamines). You may also find yourself drinking more alcohol than usual. *Nonetheless, in stage two you are conscious of what drugs, stimulants, or alcohol you take and are aware of their effects on you and why you are taking them.* They do serve to reduce tension and you are able to dispense with them when not under pressure. Above all you are not dependent on drugs to get through a normal day and do not take drugs automatically when anything goes wrong.

STAGE THREE: ANXIOUS COPING STYLES

Stage three behavior is emergency behavior in absence of real emergencies. You are constantly under pressure regardless of external realities. You have major problems in at least one sphere of behavior (work, play, or love) and you find it necessary to reorganize your behavioral repertoire in order to reduce tension. *Your freedom of action is compromised and you find yourself forced to give up much enjoyment in life because you are afraid of putting yourself in a situation you can't handle.* Nonetheless, you are still able to use your personal and mental resources—skills, interests, friends—to cope with your problems. In fact, *in stage three you are able to accomplish most tasks and at least go through the motions of normal social and economic life;* fulfilling duties and obligations to friends, family, and co-workers. *The major difference is that you are going through the motions, rather than positively reacting to yourself, others, and your life.* You do not enjoy challenges, and even though you find yourself able to satisfactorily get through even difficult situations, you prefer to restrict your activities and reduce, as far as possible, any demands that might be made upon you.

Checklist for Anxious Coping Styles

1. TENSION

Your Typical Behavior
- You have signs of tension with no apparent cause.
- Your tension level may inhibit your ability to work.

Explanation and Examples

In stage three, you experience tension and attacks of anxiety without apparent cause. Common signs are sweating, rapid breathing,

and feeling fidgety. You have these attacks not only in response to difficult situations, as in stage two, but also as
common occurrences in day-to-day living. You may find yourself suffering from headaches or muscular soreness, which
makes work painful if not impossible. *You can still do enough
to get by, but you are really only coping and not determining your
own existence.*

*In stage three you are still able to reduce tension by avoiding
unpleasant situations and by relying on positive action.* Your nervousness comes and goes and does respond, at least par-
tially, to events in your environment. You are not incapable
of experiencing moments of calm or of feeling perfectly relaxed. Such comfortable states are, however, more notice-
able by their absence than by their occurrence.

2. MOOD

Your Typical Behavior
- Your moods often last for long periods.
- You have periodic hysterical behavior, with denial of
  problems; or strong emotional expressions without ap-
  parent cause or awareness.
- You often use a hostile sense of humor (e.g., sarcasm).
- You have mild, ongoing fears and phobias.
- You take unnecessary risks to overcome your fears.
- You have specific blocked emotions (e.g., love, hate),
  resulting in flat responses.

Explanation and Examples

*In stage three your moods are an important indicator of lessened
adaptability.* Your moods last much longer than you would
normally expect. Something may happen to depress or
upset you, but instead of coming out of a depressed mood
in a few hours or days, you may be depressed for weeks.
This is the case even though pleasant events occur subse-

quently. For example, you may be depressed over an unsuccessful romantic relationship. This would be normal. If over a period of time, you also received news of an important promotion, were given a surprise party by some close friends, and won a football betting pool and still remained depressed, this would be an indication of abnormal mood behavior and a significant danger signal.

Another possible symptom would be intermittent hysterical behavior, such as irrational behavior, temper tantrums, crying fits, or strong denials of your problems and weaknesses. Hysterical behavior is that which, as seen by outsiders, is clearly an attempt to release tension by denying reality. You may not really be aware of what you are saying; you jump from feeling totally depressed to feeling suddenly elated for no apparent reason. You may read into the acts of others motives that are not there. If someone compliments you, you think that he or she is in love with you or is going to offer you a promotion. If someone is abrupt with you, you think that he or she hates you. On reflection, you might realize afterward that this is not the case, but your immediate reaction is to treat others as if this were obviously the intent behind their actions. Of course it isn't (generally), and from their perspective your behavior is somewhat hysterical.

If incidents like this occur occasionally, with friends telling you that something is wrong, you don't have to worry if you are able to understand what is going on and to control your behavior. More likely, however, in stage three you will react by protesting that nothing's the matter and that you're perfectly fine. This would be a case of "I think he doth protest too much" and further evidence of more serious emotional problems.

Another common way of dealing with stage three type mental stress is with a hostile wit or sense of humor. You use your wit to make nasty or biting comments about others, which may be humorous but are clearly aggressive and hostile. This is an effective way of releasing inner rage without totally transgressing social norms. You are able to keep yourself from physically attacking others, but the hostility of your humor belies your mood and your thoughts. You don't go around hitting or killing people, but you would like to.

An alternate way of dealing with rage or anxiety in stage three is by directing your anger against yourself. This results in mild chronic fears and phobias. A mild chronic fear might be an inability to criticize your boss or a fear of airplanes that prevents you from flying. A mild phobia might be a fear of snakes or a fear of rats, even in captivity. As long as such phobias are mild and do not affect your daily life or come up often, you are still coping with life, although perhaps a bit anxiously.

As a reaction against your fears and phobias you might demonstrate the exact opposite behavior. This would be the same pattern as denying fears and problems—the "self doth protest too much" syndrome. For example, the man who is afraid of criticizing his boss even when it is warranted, suddenly begins to insult him for no apparent reason. The person who is afraid of flying decides to take up parachute-jumping; the woman who is afraid of snakes goes to a snake farm, and so on. These would be cases of *counterphobic behavior,* and if engaged in without proper precautions and preparations, could endanger the health or well-being of the individual.

Finally, people in stage three often find their strongest emotions blocked. They are so intent on controlling their moods and their feelings that they are unable to let themselves go and express their true feelings toward someone they love or hate. Some psychologists hypothesize that so much emotional energy is being wasted in overreacting to people you don't really care about, and in exaggerating your reactions to other people who are actually quite insignificant to you, that emotionally you have nothing left for those you really care about. A common example is the employer who goes out of his way to help and be considerate of casual acquaintances but is unable to express his love to his wife or to share in her emotions. He has no trouble expressing appropriate feelings with people who are not very close to him emotionally, but has trouble establishing or maintaining intimacy with those who are. Though he may be overjoyed at an accomplishment of his spouse, he is unable to offer more than a "That's nice, dear." Again, as has been emphasized above, *in stage three there is little real enjoyment in one's accomplishments or in sharing with others. You are functioning, coping, and going through the motions but not really living with your full self.*

3. THOUGHT

Your Typical Behavior

- You have a tendency to analyze rather than experience feeling.
- You often question your own ability to feel important emotions.
- You often experience obsessive worrying about things that could happen; it brings momentary respite but doesn't lead to constructive action.

Explanation and Examples

A good example of stage three thought (and stage three behavior, in general) is that of the character Frank Fontana in the television show, "Murphy Brown." Frank is constantly stressed. He analyzes his relationships with others—"I did this, therefore he hates me" "She doesn't communicate with me, therefore she doesn't love me"—but he is seldom able to experience feelings of anger, warmth, or love. When his real feelings come up he diverts conversations to other subjects like work and sports.

Other examples of stage three thought are provided by people who question their ability to love or their ability to feel affection, hate, or any strong emotion for another. They are so wrapped up in themselves and their problems that they question their ability to interact fully with another.

A common symptom of anxious coping is circular worrying. This kind of worrying occurs quite frequently in anxiety-ridden individuals. They imagine possible malfunctions and problems, many of which are unlikely to occur. When they go on a trip they make elaborate reservations, planning their entire trip to the smallest detail. Yet they still worry that a relative will get sick, that reservations will be broken, that they will misplace their travel documents, and so forth. Most important, they don't do anything to prevent these possible occurrences (often because they're the kind of thing you can't prevent), and their worrying does not lead to positive action (for example, buying a travel pouch to keep all important documents in one place instead of just worrying about how you can be extra careful not to lose them). *Obsessive worrying is more than ordinary concern about the outcome of a possible event; it is concern that is unproductive in dealing with the external factors that actually influence events.* It is more akin to fantasizing and daydreams than to rational planning. Again, occasional instances of such worrying are normal. In stage three, however, such worrying is frequent. Persons in this phase may also experience a lot of negative self-talk. Their inner dialogue and self-judgments, what they say or think about themselves, may become quite negative.

4. ACTIVITY

Your Typical Behavior
- You are often hyperactive with no particular purpose, often accompanied by a sense of exhaustion.
- Your activity level still reduces your tension.
- You require constant inspiration or feedback in order to work well.
- There is a marked reduction in your ability to take risks.

Explanation and Examples

In stage three, activity is not fluid. There are sudden spurts of energy and periods of total inertia. A common symptom is hyperactiv-

ity that leads nowhere. You run around doing a hundred different things practically simultaneously, but doing nothing well or completely. You do not work calmly and steadily. You may have difficulty getting anything done or getting up enough enthusiasm to start new projects. Then suddenly you want to make up for your last three weeks of lethargy and start to compress into a few days, weeks of activity that you have put off. Such patterns of activity are serious danger signals that you are undergoing mental stress.

In stage three you are still in relative control of your actions. You can finish some tasks and you can work well under ideal conditions. You get some satisfaction from your work, at least a minor sense of competence or self-justification. Your work makes life easier to take. But without encouragement or a positive working environment you have difficulty keeping yourself involved with your work. *You may need constant approval and appreciation from your employer and co-workers.* You need to be reminded that your work is important or necessary and that your efforts are appreciated. You cannot work well on ambiguous projects or on tasks in which you define the goals and evaluation criteria yourself. *You need support from others and become less creative, and less independent in all your endeavors.*

This state carries over into your nonprofessional activities as well. *You find it difficult to make decisions*—even to decide what to order for dinner or where to sit in a theater or what movie to see. To some extent, occasional bouts of indecision and insecurity over your decision-making ability is normal. In stage three, such occurrences are frequent. *In stage three, you rarely take a risk or try something new.*

You are unsure of your ability to adapt to new people or new challenges and prefer to stick with the tried and true; not only in fundamental areas of your life, in which a wrong decision could be costly, but even in nonthreatening situations in which it is either not significant or not possible to make a wrong choice—where to have dinner, what shade of lipstick to wear, or where to spend your vacation.

5. ORGANIZATION/CONTROL

Your Typical Behavior

- You become increasingly rigid; you require clear-cut guidelines, or you need perfect conditions in order to function.
- You are regularly over-extended; resulting in forgetfulness, shortcuts, occasional shoddy work that can be upsetting to you or to others.
- Unpredictable events are often able to disrupt or negatively influence your performance.
- You are involved in occasional impulsive behaviors.
- Your personal rituals interfere with work (e.g., sharpening pencils).
- You have a limited capacity for self-insight and for change.

Explanation and Examples

Stage three organization and control behavior is similar to that of stage four anxious coping activity behavior. *You have little flexibility or creativity in your organizational efforts. Everything must be "just so" in order to function.* You cannot tolerate ambiguity or open-ended projects. Goals must be clearly defined; procedures clearly laid out. There is no room for innovation or unexpected modifications of demands. You want and need direct commands and clear objectives. It is not sufficient to know general goals; you need specifics in work situations and social situations as well. Before meeting someone you must know exactly what they're like and how to treat them.

Because this need for rigidity in organizing your life is almost impossible to achieve, given the fluidness and unpredictability of most of life, you often find yourself overextended, doing work that is not up to your own standards, or which is clearly not up to your sense of your potential. Because rigid organization requires planning for events that infrequently occur, much effort is wasted and you take longer to get your work done. *You often demonstrate perfectionistic behavior,* spending too much time with details that aren't really very important. As a result, you end up forgetting more significant procedures or taking shortcuts that reduce the quality of your work.

Your adaptability is reduced. Unexpected delays or last-minute changes in plans are intolerable; they completely destroy your ability to work or to enjoy yourself. If you plan a camping trip and, because of a flat tire, arrive too late to find a camping site, you become completely demoralized and unable to adjust smoothly. Eventually you are able to cope with this unforeseen difficulty (by going somewhere else, finding a motel, camping along the road, or even sleeping in the car) but only after experiencing extreme anxiety, frustration, or anger. *In stage three you are able to cope and you often hit on very good plans and solutions to difficult problems, but you are only coping and it is a painful process.* (This is in contrast to someone in stage one who might have less imagination about what to do in such a predicament but is calmer, steadier, and more confident that he'll be able to arrange some adequate alternative. In stage three you minimize your efforts and organizational abilities, while in stage one you maximize your mental and real resources.)

Occasional compulsive behavior includes reading every book on a course reading list, even though you know that it's not required or expected by your professor. Suddenly deciding to take off from work to go to the beach, buying clothes you don't really need, or suddenly deciding to dye your hair while at the beauty salon are examples of impulsive behavior. Such impulsive acts are not necessarily signs of stage three, but when they are disruptive or out of character, they are probable danger signals.

In stage three, ritualistic behavior becomes much more common. You find little rituals provide tension release. The result of these momentary defenses is, however, often disruptive or counterproductive. You spend more time clearing up your desk in preparation for work you have to do than in the actual work. You develop a series of rigid behavior patterns in which you have to go through a number of often unnecessary steps to get something done. *Your behavior becomes mechanized.* You have a set response that does not vary, even though the input does. You treat all problems as if they were identical. You are unable to adapt to the particularities and subtle differences between problems.

You have difficulty learning from experience. Because you try to force everything and everyone into set patterns, you are unable to change and to grow. Your rigid responses are incapable of perceiving individual differences. *You react to problems rather than acting on them.* You are afraid to experiment with new strategies or to stray from tried solutions. You are cautious about changing behavior patterns and seek situations with which you are comfortable and which pose few threats. You do not experiment or modify your plans or your behavior. You do not generate changes but passively react to your environment. You have difficulty in directing and defining yourself and your life. You get by, sometimes very satisfactorily, but your successes and happiness depend more on the actions of others than on any self-realizing behavior. *You feel that your life is not as full as it might be and that you are not reaching your potential.*

6. INTERPERSONAL RELATIONSHIPS

Your Typical Behavior
- You find yourself interacting with others in a compulsive, inappropriate manner.
- You must always get your own way; you're unable to compromise.
- You can be scapegoated by others, or you can be a bully.
- You often initiate one-to-one relationships that you later regret.
- You have volatile, deteriorating friendships, often featured by grudges.
- You generally need constant outside support or approval.

- You often demonstrate mild antisocial behavior or you feel alienated.

Explanation and Examples

In stage three you overreact to others. You have a need to create strong bonds with others, which is not being fulfilled. As a result you seize inappropriate moments—such as trying to make a date with a boy who is having dinner with another girl-friend—in which to try to establish contact. You expect more from casual acquaintances than most other people and try to force yourself on others. When rejected or even when your attentions are merely returned without the intensity behind your own, you become disappointed and often angry. You then go to the opposite extreme and, for some minor argument, reject entirely someone who the previous day you had hoped would become an intimate friend.

In stage three you have a compulsion to always get your own way. Everybody has to play by your rules and you regard yourself as the center of the universe. You have difficulty giving to others and seek constant signs of reassurance or of affection from those you love or respect. You become very anxious when you have to leave a set of friends or enter a new group of friends. You react as does a child when he or she first goes to school and gets very frightened, sometimes including physical symptoms, such as vomiting at the prospect of having to leave the security of the family home. In a less dramatic way you too become frightened at the prospect of separating yourself from those you have depended on in the past. Incidents may come up about changing jobs, receiving a promotion, having neighbors and family move away, and so forth.

To deal with the anxiety you feel in entering new groups you may develop extreme interpersonal stances of withdrawal or aggression. If you choose withdrawal you become passive, allowing others to order you around, make fun of you, or blame you every time anything goes wrong. By seeking such low-status roles in groups you avoid the anxiety of asserting yourself on a give-and-take basis. You don't have to fear rejection because you know you belong and the price of self-humiliation does not strike you as excessive, given your fears and inability to establish satisfying relationships in other ways. The other alternative would be to bully others into accepting you. They may accept you out of fear, but again you illustrate a stage three failing of being unable to interact with others on an equal footing.

In stage three your social life is unbalanced. You establish sudden intimacies that deteriorate and fall apart. You throw yourself into romantic relationships that you know are unlikely to survive. You consciously ignore factors about another that you know will create problems later on (inappropriate educational level, politically on the left while you are right-center, widely different interests, etc.).

Your friendships are accompanied by frequent crises. Disputes erupt often, many of them resulting in grudges of both long and short duration. You find it difficult to overlook or forgive faults in others. You seek perfection, both in yourself and in others. You have difficulty accepting actions that are generated by the frailty or weaknesses of others and try to ignore such weaknesses in yourself.

Because you have a distorted and unrealistic attitude toward the way in which people interact, substituting the ideal for the actual, you feel particularly badly when you see that you don't measure up to the standards that you hold for others. The fact that these standards are unrealistic escapes you, and you are left with a sense of worthlessness. *Instead of merely realizing that you, like everyone else, are not perfect either in thought or in deed, you overreact and feel that you are a totally worthless or inadequate person.* This sense of worthlessness penetrates even your strongest relationships with self-doubts, which can only be relieved by continual assurances of your strength, good humor, or general likability by friends, colleagues, and lovers. Often you really do possess the superior qualities you feel you show, but your inability to accept your weaknesses prevents you from feeling confident and secure. Your constant need to be petted and praised often creates tensions among those who care most about you.

Mild antisocial behavior may include selfishness, callousness to others, and overall irresponsibility. Such antisocial behavior is generally impulsive, a case of seeking personal pleasure without regard to the consequences of one's actions. More than a lack of consideration or bad manners, antisocial behavior has an undercurrent of hostility. Alienation is a general feeling of not belonging or not sharing the values of the society in which you live. You do not feel comfortable accepting that which those around you take for granted. There are many legitimate reasons, both existential and political, for feeling alienated from modern society, but *in stage three, alienation occurs not so much because you are consciously trying to create a different value system or relationship to the world, but because you are unable to fit into society as it exists. You may feel blind rage against the external world and can't identify the legitimate causes of your suffering.* By blaming society for your problems you are able to preserve the illusion that you have few internal mental problems and that unknown others are responsible for your shortcomings.

7. PHYSICAL

Your Typical Behavior
- You have many fluctuations in eating and sleeping patterns, changes in weight, and minor gastrointestinal problems.
- You have periodic skin blemishes and headaches.
- You have physical tics and/or stuttering.
- You often use drugs and alcohol or seek medical help to "feel better."
- You are involved in episodes of drug abuse, often reinforced by your friends or contacts.

Explanation and Examples

A common symptom of anxious coping behavior is chronic overeating, resulting in obesity or undereating. You eat not because you are hungry but in order to release tensions. You have little self-control about what you eat and find it impossible to refuse any food you really enjoy regardless of not feeling hungry. You become a compulsive eater, not cutting down even though you know that being overweight endangers your physical health and diminishes your ability to participate in a wide range of physical activities. You may also become less attractive.

The opposite symptom, lack of appetite, is an alternative manifestation of the same stresses that create overeaters. Not eating is a way of withdrawing and punishing yourself, just as overeating is an aggressive action against yourself. Both patterns of behavior attack your body and are important signs of inner stress. Of course, there may be purely physical reasons in some cases for overeating or lack of appetite, but in most cases they are important indicators of emotional problems.

Not being able to sleep at night, and waking up in the middle of the night or very early in the morning are also signs of inner conflicts. Chronic oversleeping is another possible indicator, usually associated with mild cases of depression.

Moderate-level gastrointestinal problems include minor problems such as stomach upset, gas, and diarrhea, which become chronic. If such ailments become permanent aspects of your digestive behavior, more serious physical problems may result.

In stage three, headaches become much more common as do hives and other types of skin rashes. Physical tics, such as always winking your eye or moving your left wrist in a particular way before speaking, may also occur. Such physical tics are unconscious and uncontrollable. You are not aware that you have these automatic responses until someone points them out to you. Sometimes they disappear naturally but they are generally related to mental stress. Stuttering in most cases is also related to nervousness and anxiety. Even when there are physical causes of the problem, the mental dimension should also be considered and treated.

A sign that your physical behavior is beginning to break down is the need to take medication just to feel better or feel right. You do not take drugs or aspirin for specific physical ailments but just to relieve general tension. You become dependent on sleeping pills and other tranquilizers or stimulants, resorting to them whenever you're feeling a little off.

Episodic or frequent use of illegal drugs, such as marijuana, is another indicator. To use such drugs occasionally, especially given the social pressures to indulge existing in many subgroups, is not necessarily indicative of mental conflicts. But when usage becomes daily or as often as three or four times a week, there are probably mental stresses involved in your usage as well. The same would be true in the case of alcohol. In both cases, you know you have problems when you can no longer control your intake of these substances.

STAGE FOUR: ANXIOUS CHARACTERS

Stage four behavior is an intensification of stage three behavior symptoms. Your anxious coping devices have become permanent parts of your personality. Your nonfunctional behavior has become consistent and predictable. Unlike stage three behavior, which can respond to positive opportunities in your environment and diminish or grow, stage four behavior continues in spite of environmental opportunities to behave differently. Even when others treat you in an ideal fashion you exhibit disruptive or destructive behavior. You do not take advantage of opportunities to grow.

Also in stage four you begin to make organizational adjustment to problem behavior. You can't really cope. Certain motions you are able to go through in stage three may stop altogether. Your problems are such that you may often abandon responsibilities, take time off from work, or restructure your daily routine in order to get through the day.

Your nonfunctional behavior is further removed from the external causes of stress. *You have internalized stressful*

*situations to the point that they occur spontaneously and are al-
most unrelated to what actually goes on in your interactions with
persons and things.* You become angry for apparently no reason. You perceive threats where none exist. You react to
what you think others want to do or say and not to what
they actually do or say.

*Your nonfunctional behavior is tenaciously and vigorously
maintained even in the face of serious resistance by others.* You do
not adapt to procedures or institutions about you, but you
expect and often cause co-workers, school friends, or others
with whom you come into contact to alter their procedures
to accommodate your special needs.

*You can reduce anxiety only by closing your cognitive field to
restrict and avoid new stimuli.* You try to take in as few new
perceptions as possible about your problems. You are unable to learn anything about your original problem because
you have lost the ability to look at yourself calmly and objec-
tively. You exaggerate and underestimate both your weaknesses and strengths. The only acceptable solution is to
choose a particular interpretation of yourself that allows you
to survive without total chaos. You want to avoid scrutiniz-
ing your behavior and your problems because you are afraid
of what you'll find; you are afraid of breaking down entirely
and being completely unable to cope.

*In stage four at least two of the three areas of life (work, love,
and play) are seriously impaired.* You may be experiencing serious problems at work, or interpersonal problems at home,
or an inability to do anything but work, sacrificing completely the areas of love and play. You may be unable to organize your behavior or control your thoughts. *Nonetheless,
often a single area, a particularly gratifying relationship, a successful career, or an enthusiastic sport or hobby enables you to cope and
function moderately well.*

*Perhaps the greatest difference between stage three and stage
four behavior is that in stage four your resources are consumed or
their use blocked.* You have reached the end of the line. You
can no longer rely on your abilities, friends, interests, and
positive strengths to get you through crises. In stage three

you are still able to help yourself. This becomes increasingly difficult in stage four. In stage three you can still get by with a little help from your friends. *In stage four you may need more formal intervention or the aid of a professional.*

Checklist for Anxious Characters

1. TENSION

Your Typical Behavior

- You may feel less ongoing tension than before due to use of strong defenses.
- You have periods of nearly unbearable anxiety with no obvious cause.

Explanation and Examples

Instead of feeling tension about trying to establish a romantic relationship you give up completely and avoid meeting or trying to establish an intimate relationship. You feel tension in going to work, so you may stop going. You have difficulty accepting a dependent role, so you become aggressive and unapproachable. You feel weak and helpless, so you exaggerate your abilities in a particular area and delude yourself with feelings of grandiosity and invincibility. *All such behavior patterns reduce your experience of tension but at the cost of distorting or limiting your view of yourself and life.*

When you give up these defenses or do not concentrate on fighting off your anxieties you may experience almost unbearable anxiety. Such attacks may have both physical and mental manifestations, from being unable to move, feeling extreme stiffness in your entire body, and having nausea and pains in the pit of your stomach, to having suicidal tendencies, experiencing macabre thoughts, and feeling that you are going to explode. *Whatever manifestations of anxiety you exhibited in the lower stages become more severe and they occur in absence of any specific cause.* You feel as if you're falling apart at the seams or that everything is on the verge of going out of control. You're in a panic and unable to reduce tension by merely relaxing or seeking normal comforts.

2. MOOD

Your Typical Behavior

- Your background moods often affect your ability to work, love, and play.
- You have ongoing depressed, unhappy states (or possible suicide attempts); no amount of support or reassurance helps.
- You may get "high" on ideas or plans, but you have problems in finishing or following through.
- Your phobias and fears affect your enjoyment and productivity.
- You have self-destructive, risk-taking behavior.
- You often have periods of hysterical behavior (e.g., tantrums and outbursts).

Explanation and Examples

You are strongly influenced by the moods of those around you. You react to changes in weather much more intensely, feeling joyful when it's sunny and morose when it's grey. If there is tension or irritability at the office (among others, not involving you), you find yourself unable to work effectively. Sentimental songs make you sad, angry songs make you angry, and these emotions carry over to your activities. *You are more susceptible to moodiness than in previous stages.*

You may be chronically depressed or experience a general feeling of doom and despair. Or you can become nihilistic, wanting to destroy everything and everybody, delighting in the contemplation that ultimately everything will be destroyed and no human accomplishment will remain. Your general pessimism, uncertainty, apathy, or sadness is not diminished even when those you care about comfort you and reassure you of your worth. You feel that you and all your efforts are meaningless failures, and this feeling does not disappear even when contradicted by those in a position to judge. *In stage three you may have exhibited similar feelings of despair but your depression was affected and mitigated by your friends. In stage four nothing seems to help.* Your conflicts are too complicated and too weighty. You feel that no one can understand you and that praise or comfort cannot alleviate your problems.

When you do come out of your depression you may get "high" on ideas or plans. You become elated and super-enthusiastic, almost as if on a drug trip. Your thinking goes very fast, and you have insights into yourself and others that you never had before. You feel that you have finally found solutions to what had seemed insurmountable problems. Or you may have an idea for a project at work or a social event for which you begin to make elaborate plans. You are bubbling over with enthusiasm and energy. You talk about your plans with others and they seem genuinely impressed and supportive of your good ideas. But the crunch comes in following through or finishing these projects. The tremendous enthusiasm that you originally had suddenly disappears. Where at the start you overstated the importance of your insights or projects, you now devalue them entirely. Somehow you no longer understand how you could have gotten so excited. Your ideas no longer seem so brilliant, and you lose faith in your abilities. You go back into a low until another high comes along, repeating the pattern.

Phobias and fears prevent you from enjoying yourself or working effectively. Past failures or situations seem destined to repeat themselves. Even when things are going well, you are frightened that a disaster will strike or that some basic personality flaw will be revealed and catch you up in a humiliating or destructive failure. *To counteract these fears, you purposely put yourself in difficult situations in which you will be called upon to exhibit the opposite of what is normal for you.* As a result, you practically ensure your failure from the start by your own selection. Examples include a timid man walking into a bar in which he knows he will get into a fight he can't win, and a woman who is afraid of being assaulted walking alone at night in a dangerous part of the city. More sophisticated examples would include any behavior in which you are going out of your way to make life difficult for yourself by trying to be what you're not. You provoke precisely the kind of situations that are most painful for you and most destructive for your self-image and sense of well-being.

In stage four you may also exhibit predictable hysterical behavior. You may construct situations unconsciously that permit you to alleviate your inner anxieties with hysterical outbursts and temper tantrums. You may experience fits of destructibility in which you do injury to property, yourself, or others. Or you may become super-impressionable, changing your fundamental beliefs from one day to the next, depending on the persons and stimuli around you. All such behavior is indicative of inner stresses that can no longer be contained and that seek external release.

3. THOUGHT

Your Typical Behavior

- You often have chronic distortions of reality.
- You are often alert to an unspecified danger.
- You are suspicious; you continually overinterpret insignificant pieces of information.
- You are often blind to important facts.
- You have repetitive, bothersome thoughts that disrupt your living.
- You are often unable to experience specific feelings (e.g., love, anger).
- You have great difficulty in making decisions.

Explanation and Examples

Overpersonalizing events is manifested when you interpret external events in terms of yourself. For instance, you may feel that whether your favorite sports team wins or loses is a reflection on your emotional participation as a television viewer. Or you may make a connection between the outbreak of a fire or a plane crash with some private personal thought or event. Alternatively, you may have a single explanatory system for all occurrences, such as astrology, in which you distort your perceptions of reality in order to conform to a single model of the universe. You may have a private code or explanation that enables you to make sense of inexplicable events.

A feeling of paranoia is also characteristic of anxious characters. You are suspicious of yourself and others. You overinterpret insignificant events. You call someone up and she's not there, and you interpret this to mean that she doesn't want to speak to you or that she doesn't like you. Or a friend fails to return your greeting in the street, and you automatically assume he's trying to ignore you rather than assume that he merely didn't see you, which is probably the case.

Deficiency in knowledge means that you are blind to certain facts. You fail to gather sufficient information and are unaware of the gaps in your knowledge concerning both concrete situations and abstract relationships. You develop mental blocks that prevent you from utilizing your full range of problem-solving techniques. Even when these facts are pointed out, you are unable to understand or retain them.

You may have repetitive bothersome thoughts that actually disrupt your work or your relationships. You may have continuous sexual fantasies that distract you completely from communicating with others. Religious thoughts, fears, or strong visual images may constantly impinge upon your thinking, making problem-solving or analytical thought impossible.

Your thoughts may so preoccupy you that specific feelings are completely blocked. You are unable to relate to another person with your full attention, and strong emotions such as love, comradery, or anger fail to appear.

Perhaps the clearest indication of stage four thought behavior is a total breakdown of your ability to make decisions. You have difficulty processing information. You go over the same facts again and again without analyzing which factors you should concentrate on. You have difficulty in focusing on specific problems and issues. Your thinking goes round and round without advancing. Alternatively, you finally do think a problem through, arrive at a good solution, but abandon it in order to go through the process to arrive at another, and another, and another. You are full of doubts and always imagine that there is a better choice than those of which you are currently aware. You don't know when to stop gathering information. *All decisions, even minor ones, seem of vital importance.* In the end, you find yourself incapable of making a rational decision and act impulsively, later regretting the consequences and blaming yourself for not having stuck to your original choice of action.

4. ACTIVITY

Your Typical Behavior
- You generally avoid new activities.
- Your activities no longer succeed in relieving your tension.
- Your activities are usually solitary, you engage in them seriously, and they give you no particular pleasure in accomplishment.

Explanation and Examples

In stage four you avoid all new activities as far as possible. You find mere survival taxing and feel that your energies are tapped to the limit. You do not really enjoy life or activities. They give you no sense of competence, purpose, or meaning. You are frightened that if you don't continue to go to work, talk to people, or go out occasionally you will go completely mad, but you do not experience positive satisfaction in your accomplishments.

In every act, you see a life-and-death struggle. Every defeat or failure is a sign that you are going under; your successes are signs that you are still surviving. You cannot afford to do something frivolously or lightly. You must conserve your energy for important activities because you feel you have so little of it. Your feeling of doom or worthlessness is not alleviated by your activities.

5. ORGANIZATION/CONTROL

Your Typical Behavior

- Your behavior is often very mechanical.
- Unexpected minor events often cause you to stop work, or to stop the activities of love and play.
- You find yourself doing obsessive rituals in order to function.
- You often display impulsive behavior that disrupts your plans or relationships, and you don't learn from your mistakes or experience.

Explanation and Examples

In stage four you behave in a very mechanical manner, to be totally certain of always making the same response and doing the same action. You envy the routine and total structure in which a machine operates—you know exactly what is expected of you, you don't have to cope with any human factors or uncertainties, you do not have to set your own pace or create your own work procedures—at least this is how you might imagine your ideal work situation.

In your daily life, unexpected events completely throw you. A traffic delay, a detour, or getting lost all become major catastrophes accompanied by anxiety, anger, or temper displays. On a date you try to plan every detail and if anything goes wrong you become extremely anxious and consider the date spoiled. Other examples would include walking off the court in tennis when your partner fails to keep his proper position, going into a rage when finding a typing mistake in letters you dictated, or becoming morose, irritable, or angry upon learning that a movie or sporting event you had planned on seeing is sold out. When such minor deviations not only bother you but destroy your sense of balance and ability to carry out or formulate plans, your behavior is clearly that of a well-established anxious character.

In stage four you cannot tolerate any deviance. You try to plan every stage and event of your life. To protect yourself from variations or "mistakes" you develop set formulae for handling situations, people, and work projects. You may often need to go through extensive rituals in order to function. These rituals consist of idiosyncratic stylized behavior. *The use of rituals by themselves is not of an anxious character, but obsessive dependence upon them is.*

Another possible symptom would be impulsive behavior that disrupts plans. Again, the clue is not impulsive behavior *alone,* which sometimes can be refreshing, but the disruptive effects of your impulses. You may painstakingly organize a system for retrieving information and then one day impulsively decide not to use it, throwing your files into chaos. *A most important indicator of stage four would be the inability to learn from experience or your mistakes.* If you make the same organizational errors again and again, something is wrong. You should be able to modify your procedures and exercise sufficient self-control in order to improve upon your performance in work, love, and play. *You are not able, in stage four, to avoid re-creating negative environments or repeating inadequate responses.*

6. INTERPERSONAL RELATIONSHIPS

Your Typical Behavior

- You show continued withdrawal or aggression toward friends and peers, resulting in some abandonment.
- You have extreme dependency on others and a strong need to manipulate others.
- You often hold extreme grudges against others.

Explanation and Examples

Your interpersonal problems are basically the same as those in stage three but more severe. You continue to withdraw from friends, either physically or emotionally. You think up excuses for avoiding colleagues and associates. If you go to a party you try to stay to the side, not involving yourself with others. An alternative, but similar manifestation, would be to exhibit extreme hostility when approached by others. In either case, you signal that you want to be left alone, and this is generally the result achieved as some friends cease to associate with you.

In stage four you become extremely dependent on a few key people. You feel that you can't live without them and will do anything to maintain their loyalty or their availability. *Depending upon the personalities of those upon whom you are dependent, you may either be easily manipulated by them, or find yourself manipulating them in order to maintain a hold on them.* Such manipulative behavior creates strains in your relationships, and they may often break up in dramatic and sometimes violent confrontations. *You do not easily forgive even minor betrayals, and you may harbor permanent grudges.*

7. PHYSICAL

Your Typical Behavior

- You display a stiffness and contraction in your physical mannerisms.
- You have chronic psychosomatic problems—ulcers, colitis, insomnia, migraines, absence of menses, anorexia, chronic overeating—*in the absence of a clear-cut cause.*
- You are involved in chronic solitary drug or alcohol abuse, as a coping mechanism or self-medication.
- You experience continual exhaustion.

Explanation and Examples

Physical mannerisms refer to common voluntary and involuntary movements such as walking, reaching, talking, eating, and the like. Walking with a heavy step, as if drugged, and displaying stiffness and tightness in your muscles and body movements are examples.

Chronic psychosomatic problems refer to problems that have both a physical and mental component and persist over long periods of time, longer than would be expected for solely physically caused problems. All of the psychosomatic problems listed above may also occur normally as a result of specific external causes such as diet, drugs, and organic deterioration. However, when they occur inexplicably without a clear-cut physical or environmental cause, they are probably signs of the extreme mental stress associated with stage four.

Ulcers usually form in the digestive tract of the stomach. They are extremely painful and are aggravated by certain diets of spicy or fatty foods, and by eating too fast. Colitis is an inflammation of the colon. It may become painful to make bowel movements and may produce blood in your stools. Both of these conditions should be treated by medical specialists.

Migraines are severe headaches that may persist for days and recur frequently. Insomnia is the inability to fall asleep. Absence of menses refers to a woman's failure to experience a normal menstrual flow. Anorexia refers to a prolonged avoidance of food. In severe cases, malnutrition and anemia result. Extreme obesity and overeating would be comparable symptoms of stage four physical behavior. *Again, it should be recalled that a single anxious character trait does not place you in stage four.* This is especially true of physical symptoms that can often have other causes. Nonetheless, the presence of these symptoms is well worth investigating as possible signs of emotional distress.

Other physical traits include dependence on drugs for daily survival in response to mental and not physical conditions. This is especially true of drugs or alcohol taken alone and not in the company of others as a social act. Alcoholism and habitual drug abuse are associated with stage four.

Finally, sheer exhaustion, especially when not accompanied by perceivable mental or physical activity, is an important danger signal. *Constant feelings of tiredness and exhaustion that are not linked to physical diseases are a sign of great interior mental stress and mental conflicts.*

STAGE FIVE: DISTURBED BEHAVIOR

Stage five is that of major mental illnesses (or emotional distress) that should be treated as soon as possible. Stage five behavior is that of lowest adaptability. People in stage five can usually no longer function adequately as members of society. Their inner conflicts consume all of their available energy, and they have exhausted their strengths and positive resources for coping.

Within stage five there is probably as wide a range of behavior variation as in the first four stages combined. Severe cases require institutionalization. Milder problems could be dealt with in the home atmosphere.

General attributes of stage five behavior include disrupted living patterns in all three areas of life (work, love, and play), an inability to care for oneself, and gross distortions of reality or hallucinations. In stage five there is also a complete dependency on others. There is no stability. There are frequent and major breakdowns in all areas of life. There is not, as commonly exists in stage four, one saving area of competence and fulfillment that enables the individual to survive and to cope. You no longer see certain aspects of the world as those around you do, and you have difficulty in communicating what you see and what you feel.

As a result, a common symptom of stage five behavior is chronic, severe conflict with parents, friends, school, and/or the law. You have special needs and are unable to adapt to the needs of others. You live in a world of your own with special dangers and rewards, and when others impinge on these highly charged and special domains, you can no longer coordinate your behavior with theirs.

In stage five you do things that other people consider very disturbed. You may see, hear, or feel things of which others aren't aware. You may experience feelings of private ecstasy, which you are unable to communicate or control. You may believe that you are someone or something you're not. You may no longer perceive danger to your physical body, feeling that you have transcended yourself. You may expose yourself to dangers without realizing it, or attempt suicide (perceived by you as suicide against a part of your personality in order that an imagined new self may be born instead).

The list of possible disorders and manifestations of disturbed behavior is endless. Particular perceptions may actually pertain to a "higher realm" of being or spirit above that of the everyday world. Real insights into significant extrasensory states may exist. Nonetheless, from the point of view of the everyday world these insights are too abstract or isolating to be useful. The difference between being a madman and a genius is the ability to control and communicate. *In stage five you cannot control your behavior, and you cannot make others understand you. Stage five persons are unable (not just unwilling) to live in our everyday world.*

Checklist for Disturbed Behavior

1. TENSION

Your Typical Behavior
- Your tension feels unbearable in the absence of medication.
- Your tension is relieved only by disturbed thinking (distortions, hallucinations, grossly inappropriate plans).

Explanation and Examples

In stage five you often feel as if you're going to explode. Your anxieties completely drain you. Neither work nor play nor any normal everyday activity relieves your tension. You can function only in response to drugs when experiencing these states of anxiety. Even frenetic behavior—running around doing many tasks, taking care of many concerns that seem to be creating your anxieties—fails to help.

In addition to taking medication, you may find yourself distorting reality in order to relieve tension. For example, if you are anxious about your inability to pay your bills you may convince yourself that you are going to receive a large inheritance from a nonexistent benefactor. You may also deal with unpleasant situations by imagining that they do not exist or that you have friends or voices that will come to your aid. Whenever you are tense, these images, sights, or sounds will appear. Insofar as no one else can perceive or share these realities, they are called hallucinations.

Other disturbed thinking that may appear is the resolution of conflicts by grandiose or clearly inappropriate plans. Recorded cases include an unemployed guitarist writing to the Beatles for an audition, and an acting student who planned on getting the lead role in a film that had already been made. A common manifestation is resolving failed interpersonal and romantic relationships by planning to establish an intimate relationship with some famous or far-off figure whom you don't even know. In all cases, large miracle solutions and plans are made to deal with personal crises that you find yourself unable to accept or deal with in a practical and realistic fashion. Rather than admitting your inability and weaknesses, you make fantastic plans that serve as reassurances that you are a very special and successful individual. The plans are usually of such a nature that it is impossible even to begin to carry them out, and failure to do so can be attributed to any number of external factors that do not reflect upon your own inadequacies and real conflicts and problems.

2. MOOD

Your Typical Behavior

- You are often flooded with feelings unrelated to reality.
- You have manic behavior, frequently accompanied by delusions, ideas of reference, and distortions of reality.

- You have severely depressed moods; you are unable to work or to love; you are unreachable.
- You experience thought disorders, or hallucinations.

Explanation and Examples

In stage five, moods come upon you suddenly with no recognizable cause. Strong feelings surge from within and dominate your mood. These feelings are so strong that they counteract stimuli in the everyday world that normally account for your different moods.

Manic behavior is that which is characterized by drastic changes in mood from one extreme of elation and hyperactivity to the opposite extreme of depression and inactivity. One moment you have high hopes, enthusiasm, and the feeling that you can't fail and hours later you are apathetic, skeptical, and fearful of embarrassing yourself. In most cases, both the elation and the depression are uncalled-for or inappropriate responses to what is actually going on around you. These responses are often accompanied by *delusions* (firmly held false beliefs). These delusions may be either paranoid (feeling persecuted or victimized), leading to depression, or protective (anonymous benefactor), leading to elation. An example of a delusion leading to manic behavior would be the elated behavior of a man who believed he was about to be given an important government post, although his actual occupation was that of a file clerk.

Ideas of reference and distortions of reality are similar to delusions. Ideas of reference that are inappropriate are often associated with manic mood changes. For example, interpreting a song lyric as having been written or intended to explain your behavior or that of someone close to you is a case of a misconceived point of reference. A distortion of reality is a milder form of a delusion. There is some basis for your beliefs, but they are generally out of line: Your pretty co-worker actually does feel friendly toward you (though without the erotic overtones that you perceive); you may actually be eligible for an important government job, but at some later stage of your career.

In stage five, a depressed mood brings a total halt to your ability to work, love, or play. You are unable to enjoy yourself, and your mood does not change even when what you want most is offered or given to you. This may be true even when the situation or circumstance that produced your depression is totally removed. If you are depressed because you thought your girlfriend had left you for another and she hadn't, or because you had received an incorrect message concerning your financial position, which is stronger than you had thought, and you remain depressed after learning of these favorable events, you are suffering from depression. If all your friends try to cheer you up and can't; if no one seems able to relieve you of your problems or enable you to think of more pleasant subjects, then you would be psychologically unreachable and in need of professional guidance.

Severe depression and mood shifts are often associated with thought disorders and hallucinations. Hallucinations are sensory experiences not shared by others. They are produced by no stimuli or by stimuli that others do not perceive. As far as the rest of the world is concerned, you are seeing or hearing things. Hallucinations can be associated with your deep moods, insofar as your moods overwhelm your senses and heighten your experiences. For example, when elated you may be feeling so high that you see golden rays emanating from people you love. When depressed you may feel black beasts fighting in your gut and actually hear them shouting and struggling.

Thought disorders may be considered cases of faulty thinking. Your positive or negative moods are so strong that you block out information that is incompatible with your present mood. You overlook facts and distort others as you are carried along by a single overpowering feeling or view of the world. *In this state your thinking is often fuzzy and your judgment is very unreliable.*

3. THOUGHT

Your Typical Behavior

- You have continual obsessive thoughts.
- You have gross perceptual distortions (i.e., you do not see, hear, or feel what others do).

Explanation and Examples

Stage five thought manifests itself in all of the disorders of stage four and more. Obsessive thoughts become frequent. Obsessive thoughts are those which you hold even when they are clearly inappropriate. They do not leave you alone; you cannot get them out of your mind. Certain questions, ideas, or desires may become obsessive. You can become obsessed with the idea of writing a book, of making love to a certain woman, or of solving the riddle of the meaning of life. In all three cases it is a good bet that your obsessive thought is either an impossible desire or a goal toward which you make no constructive effort. You always think of writing a best-seller but never actually sit down and write at all. The woman you want to make love to is married to a famous actor and lives 2000 miles away. It is impossible to solve the riddle of the meaning of life. Curiosity or mild concern with such thoughts from time to time would not be abnormal. *What is abnormal is the intensity with which stage five persons cling to such thoughts.* They never stop contemplating the same issues over and over again. They become oblivious to other people and other ideas and are unable to redirect their energies, thoughts, and desires to other, more easily obtainable subjects and goals.

Insofar as stage five persons are unable to satisfy their desires in the everyday world they retreat further into a private fantasy world in which their desires are fulfilled. This may result in gross perceptual distortions. Their psyches can no longer tolerate the continual barrage on their private fantasy world that contact with the "real" world produces. To deal with this conflict between their perceptions of the world with their eyes, ears, and other senses and the idealized world of thoughts and fantasies they carry within, they begin to resort to *distortions*. They no longer see what they don't want to see. They distort images so that they will agree with their private vision of how the world ought to be. Sometimes this private world can be terrifying and painful. Yet the realization that the world is not as the severely disturbed person imagines may be more terrifying still. It is important to point out that such perceptual distortions are usually quite specific. *For the most part the severely disturbed person thinks and perceives as well as any normal person. He or she is not retarded. Major portions of the disturbed person's personality do remain intact. But, there are certain key areas in which his or her perceptions and thinking processes break down.* These areas are in conflict with obsessive thoughts, and with his or her private fantasy world. For every disturbed person, these areas will be different and unique and ultimately they will correspond with real problems and conflicts that have produced these fantasy worlds.

4. ACTIVITY

Your Typical Behavior

- You are frequently engaged in compulsive, ritualistic activity.
- You have extreme difficulty in changing your patterns of activity.

Explanation and Examples

Compulsive ritualistic activity is that which is repeated over and over again despite its inappropriateness or lack of connection to reality. The activity is rigid and totally self-contained. It may start as a normal desire for hygiene and cleanliness and end as ritualistic handwashing that is performed a hundred or more times a day. *In stage five, these rituals no longer facilitate work or reduce tension. They have become an end in themselves and an obsession.* You feel that you cannot rest until a certain rite is performed but no sooner are you finished than you begin to prepare yourself to start your ritualistic behavior all over again.

In stage five whatever activity patterns you may have come to follow are extremely difficult to change. This includes normal activity. You need a very definite routine. When your routine is disrupted, you are frightened that your worst moods and compulsions will overcome you. You have no desire to take on new activities, and although you may be very unhappy, you feel that the goal is to repeat the acts of yesterday, for in this way at least things won't get worse. *In stage five, this reluctance to engage in new activities is severe.* Safe and obviously enjoyable new opportunities such as dinner invitations, parties, and trips are turned down because of your uneasiness in deviating from set motions and activities. *You are at the lowest level of adaptability and cannot even adapt to positive changes in your environment.*

5. ORGANIZATION/CONTROL

Your Typical Behavior
- You have very little self-control; you are easily influenced by external suggestion or internal feelings.
- You are so controlled by your feelings that work is almost impossible.
- You are involved in disturbing impulsive behavior.

Explanation and Examples

In stage five you have little self-control. In severely disturbed states you have none; not even control over your evacuatory movements and basic bodily functions. In less severe cases you still retain some self-control, but are easily influenced and directed by outside stimuli and uncontrollable inner feelings. You may still be able to initiate a project you want to work on and you enjoy doing but will be unable to continue if someone suggests that you should stop and do something else. You have no confidence in your plans and lose a sense of your self. You react to moods and other people's desires and are unable to follow through on activities or ideas.

In order to accomplish anything, the setting must be "just right." You must be feeling in the right mood, the weather must be perfect, your friends must also be in the same mood, and you must have the perfect ingredients in order to enjoy a garden party, for example. The same perfect conditions are necessary for successful work and lovemaking. *Since these perfect conditions seldom exist, you withdraw from many activities.* The most important ingredients are your mood and your inner feelings. Since these are seldom just right for the occasion, you begin to shape the occasion to them. The result is impulsive behavior, directed and dictated by your moods and feelings. No one, including yourself, knows what mood you are going to be in. No one can predict your behavior and you act without regard to the appropriateness of the situation or the feelings of others. Since conditions are never perfect, you abandon concern with any but internal factors and become oblivious to the outside world. *In stage four, such impulsive behavior can be disruptive to self and others. In stage five, it almost always is.*

6. INTERPERSONAL RELATIONSHIPS

Your Typical Behavior

- You live in a world of your own, unable to relate realistically to others.
- You are involved in frequent sociopathic behavior (e.g., habitual lying, cheating, stealing, and physical attacks).

Explanation and Examples

Autism is a psychological term that refers to the inability of an individual to relate to external stimuli. Examples of autistic behavior are the inability to talk, the inability to engage in social behavior, or the response to stimuli that others can't perceive. Autism is the absorption in fantasy as an escape from reality. In the interpersonal sphere this produces a breakdown of social relationships. The autistic individual does not respond to others as they are, but as he imagines them in his fantasies. An autistic individual may persist in amorous advances to a woman who has clearly rejected him on many occasions. In more severe cases of autism, communication breaks down entirely, and no one is able to understand acts and movements that take on a bizarre and totally unique aspect.

Sociopathic behavior is extreme antisocial behavior. Such behavior is characteristic of individuals who will stop at nothing to satisfy their needs and desires. They show no concern for others or for conventional morality and do not experience guilt feelings even after blatantly and ruthlessly hurting relatives or friends. As a consequence, they seldom maintain friendships for long and are often loners. *The dominant theme in interpersonal relationships for the sociopath is hostility.* This hostility may take many forms and is characterized by a total disregard for the presence and feelings of others. *Examples of sociopathic behavior include habitual lying, stealing, cheating, and physical attacks against others. In stage five, such antisocial behavior is not modified even in the face of negative feedback.* For example, a man who constantly lies, whose lies are found out, who is subsequently punished for his lies, and who in the face of severe punishments, legal action, and ostracism by his friends continues to lie, displays sociopathic behavior. More serious cases include harassment of neighbors, physical assaults, violent robberies and, in the most extreme case, murder.

7. PHYSICAL

Your Typical Behavior
- You display bizarre physical posturing (i.e., body movements that appear strange).
- You have many physical problems and a very unhealthy lifestyle.

- You have serious addictions (drug and alcohol, sexual behavior, eating disorders, etc.).

Explanation and Examples

Bizarre physical posturing refers to staring, and hand, leg, or body trunk movements that are clearly strange and out of the ordinary. For example, constant intense staring that is not modified in the face of normal social constraints is bizarre behavior. Tight muscles and always standing at a severe angle as if on the verge of falling down would be another example of bizarre physical posturing. *Any deviance in normal body control that is not the result of physical abnormality would be included in stage five physical behavior.*

Many physical problems include all of those listed in stage four and others. *Stage five individuals generally don't feel well physically, adapt lifestyles that are not conducive to sound physical health, are accident-prone, and take a long time to recover from normal illnesses.* The precise relationship between physical and mental problems is still unknown, but scientists are discovering ever greater feedback mechanisms between physical and mental factors, including the relationship between hormone production and chemical processes and emotional states and behavior syndromes.

Finally, outright addictions are signs of severely disturbed physical behavior. These addictions may take different forms, from addiction to alcohol, or everyday aspirin, to heroin. The point about addictions is that they are signals of a complete breakdown in control over your physical person. You are dependent on certain substances and your body can't function without them. *An addicted individual has reached the lowest level of adaptability, because he is incapable of adapting to any environment in which the substance to which he is addicted is absent.*

Congratulations, you have completed the Theory of the Five Stages!

Appendix B

A Mental Health Fact Sheet[11]

The following lists contain just a few of the staggering, statistics on mental health.

THE HUMAN COST OF MENTAL ILLNESS

• *The full spectrum of all mental disorders affects 22 percent of the adult population in a given year.* (This figure refers to all mental disorders, including drug- and alcohol-related problems.)

• *Mental illnesses are more common than cancer, diabetes, arthritis, or heart disease.*

• *In a given year, 10.9 percent of the population seek some mental health treatment; half of them meet criteria for an existing mental disorder.* Fortunately, less than 7 percent have symptoms for a full year or longer.

• Prevalence rates for major mental illness in adults in any one year:

Schizophrenia: 2 million
Manic depression: 2.2 million
Major depression: 9.2 million

Panic disorder: 2.4 million
Phobia: 20.1 million
Obsessive/Compulsive: 3.9 million

• Where people seek and obtain care for mental disorders: 43 percent go to their doctors or to hospitals, 40 percent go to mental health providers and clinics, 28 percent go to the voluntary health sector (non-profit agencies and clinics). (Note: People in this survey responded to more than one category.)

• Major depression is among the most common of all clinical problems encountered by primary care physicians.

• Depressive disorders, including major depression and manic depressive illness (bipolar disorder), are very common and range widely in degree of severity.

• *In a given year, 2.1 percent of the population, about 5 million Americans, suffer from depressive disorders.*

• The number one reason for hospital admissions nationwide is psychiatric disorder. At any moment almost 21 percent of all hospital beds are filled by people with mental illness.

• Schizophrenia is a severe mental illness, a brain disease that often strikes young people between ages 16 and 25. It is a thought disorder that causes some people to experience delusions and auditory and visual hallucinations. It is believed to be biological in nature, caused by genetic or viral factors.

• In a given year, nearly 2 million Americans over age 18 suffer from schizophrenia.

• Children suffer from the same range of mental disorders (including schizophrenia, depressive disorders, obsessive/compulsive disorders, and panic disorders) as do adults.

• In a given year, 3.2 percent of children and adolescents between ages 9 and 17 are diagnosed with a severe mental illness. *Only about one-third of the children and adolescents who need treatment receive it, and many may not be getting the care most appropriate to their condition.*

• *A majority of the 30,000 Americans who commit suicide each year suffer from a mental or addictive disorder.* Suicide is the second leading cause of death for teenagers ages 15 to 19; it is the third leading cause for those ages 15 to 24.

• Nearly one-third of all homeless people have a severe mental illness.

• People with mental illness are stigmatized. They are often feared and stereotyped as dangerous, aggressive, or violent. In fact, they are more likely to be isolated, passive, and withdrawn. Often, they are blamed for their illness.

They are denied opportunities to rebuild their lives because of discrimination in housing, employment, and health insurance coverage.

THE ECONOMIC COSTS OF MENTAL ILLNESS

• *In 1990 the nation's health-care bill was $670 billion; the direct cost of treating all mental disorders was 10%, or $67 billion.*

• Severe mental disorders: total direct treatment costs are $20 billion per year, plus $7 billion for long-term nursing home care. Indirect and related costs bring the total for severe mental disorders to $74 billion per year.

• One quarter of all Social Security Disability payments are for individuals with severe mental illness.

• *Depression* (including major depression, manic depression, dysthymia) *costs the American economy $43.7 billion annually.*

• Lithium (the major drug for manic-depressive disorder) has saved the United States economy more than $40 billion since 1970: $13 billion in direct treatment costs and $27 billion in indirect costs.

• Somatic symptoms of panic disorders are confusing even to doctors, leading to unnecessary expenditures. Angiograms performed because of symptoms such as racing heartbeat, difficulty in breathing, and so forth cost more than $32 million each year.

THE GOOD NEWS
ABOUT MENTAL ILLNESS

• *More effective treatments and medications are now available than ever before, covering the full range of mental and emotional problems, from mild to severe.* Some form of therapy plus medication seems to be the most powerful combination.

• Treatment success rates: for schizophrenia, 60 percent; for manic-depressive disorder, 80 percent; for major depression, 65 percent. The success rate for milder mental and emotional problems is, of course, higher. Comparatively, the success rate for treatments of heart disease ranges from 41 to 52 percent.

Appendix C

Where to Go for Help: A Resource Directory*

If you've decided that you, or someone you know, might benefit from a little help, we encourage you to make the most of the many resources that are fortunately available throughout our country. Whether you live in a city, a suburb, or a rural area, you can now receive help. We, the authors, believe there is nothing more important than your mental health and emotional well-being. We think it's better to seek counseling B.C. (before crisis) rather than A.D. (after disaster). In any event, we suggest that a little help at the right time can make a big difference in your life. We know that it can have a great affect on how you feel, as well as on how well you function. *Life is too short and too precious to suffer needlessly.*

Please remember that there are many good helping resources. These may include any of the following:

---

*For a complete guide to self-help organizations contact: American Self-Help Clearinghouse, St. Clares—Riverside Medical Center, 25 Pocono Road, Denville, NJ 07834, Telephone: 201-625-7101. Call or write to order *The Self-Help Source Book: Finding and Forming Mutual Aid Self-Help Groups.*

- Physicians
- Health maintenance organizations (HMOs)
- Community mental health centers
- Hospital departments of psychiatry and outpatient psychiatry clinics
- University or medical school–affiliated programs
- State hospital outpatient clinics
- Family service/social service agencies
- Private clinics
- Employee assistance programs
- Clergy

The following organizations represent the largest national mental health associations, and the largest groups of mental health providers who are licensed and trained in different specialties. The mental health associations provide important and necessary information for people with various mental or emotional problems. Depending on your interest, you may contact any of these organizations for more information about mental health, and for referrals to local providers in your area. If you are concerned about getting competent professionals who have met certain standards for certification, these groups might be a good place to begin seeking help.

These organizations can also provide both free information and free referrals. Please realize that many of these organizations overlap and help some of the same groups but in different ways. Also note that many have toll-free 800 numbers.

NATIONAL MENTAL HEALTH ASSOCIATIONS

The Anxiety Disorders Association of America (ADAA)
6000 Executive Blvd.
Rockville, MD 20852
Telephone: 301-231-9350
President: Jerilyn Ross

ADAA's purpose is to promote the prevention and cure of anxiety disorders and to improve the lives of all people who suffer from them. Its members include individuals with anxiety disorders, clinicians, and researchers. Founded in 1980 as the Phobia Society of America, it expanded its scope in 1990 to include the full range of anxiety disorders.

According to an M.I.T. study (1990), over 11 million Americans suffered from some form of affective disorders. Members receive information and a nationwide listing of centers, trained therapists, and self-help groups who treat these conditions: generalized anxiety disorder, obsessive-compulsive disorder, post-traumatic stress disorder, agoraphobia, and all other phobias.

Depression and Related Affective Disorders Association, Inc. (DRADA)
Meyer 3-181
600 North Wolf Street
Baltimore, MD 21287-7381
Telephone: 410-955-4647
Executive Director: Paul Hoagberg

DRADA, established in 1986, seeks to alleviate the suffering caused by clinical depression and manic depression, by providing education, information, and support services to all those struggling with these illnesses (including patients, their families, and friends). Working in cooperation with the Johns Hopkins University School of Medicine, DRADA unites patients, family members, and mental health professionals in the following ways:

- Educates the public on the biochemical cause of mania or depression
- Provides training and guidance to 55 mutual self-help support groups
- Provides an awareness program to schools, and addresses the problem of depressive illness in the workplace
- Co-sponsors an annual research symposium that attracts over 700 people, publishes a quarterly newsletter, and holds quarterly meetings that focus on specific topics related to the illness.

DRADA has grown in size to over 800 members, the majority of whom reside in the area of Maryland and Delaware, Washington, D.C., Northern Virginia, and parts of Southern Pennsylvania. However, the DRADA outreach is not limited to this area, as it provides information and support in a personalized way to persons throughout the country who either call or write for assistance.

DEPRESSION Awareness, Recognition, and Treatment (D/ART)
　Program
National Institute of Mental Health (NIMH)
5600 Fishers Lane, Room 10-85
Rockville, MD 20857
Telephone: For program information: 301-443-4140
　　　　　　For brochures: 1-800-421-4211
Director: Isabel Davidoff

NIMH's D/ART Program was launched in 1988 to bring to the general public and health and mental health care providers science-based knowledge about manic-depressive and other depressive disorders—their symptoms, diagnosis, and treatments. Sponsored by the National Institute of Mental Health, D/ART's national education program is working to reduce the tragic—and frequently unnecessary—suffering of individuals and families by encouraging early recognition of symptoms of mood disorder and use of appropriate treatment. It organizes citizens' advocacy groups and works with major corporations to develop approaches to manage depression in the workplace.

The National Alliance for the Mentally Ill (NAMI)
2101 Wilson Boulevard, Suite 302
Arlington, VA 22201
Telephone: 1-800-950-NAMI
Executive Director: Laurie Flynn

NAMI is a voluntary charitable organization that works to change the way America thinks about mental health and mental illness. Based in Arlington, Virginia, this grass-roots self-help education and advocacy organization is a referral service for patients and their families. It connects patients to sources of professional help and personal support in their areas and provides free literature about all mental illnesses.

　　NAMI was founded in 1979 by 54 people from around the country—members of local support organizations—because they felt the need to form a national organization focusing on people with mental illnesses. Most of them were family members of patients who were feeling burdened by the lack of community facilities, long-term care, and insurance for the mentally ill. Today NAMI has 140,000 members whose contributions total $1 million every year. NAMI's board is comprised only of patients or their family members.

National Depressive and Manic-Depressive Association (NDMDA)
730 North Franklin Street, Suite 501
Chicago, IL 60620
Telephone: 1-800-82 NDMDA
Executive Director: Susan Dime-Meenan

National DMDA strives to enlighten those lost in the maze of symptoms, doctors, and alienation; to guide those in the medical field toward a better understanding of their patients' problems and needs; and to eliminate the harmful effects of stigma and discrimination that are so prevalent in our society today.

National DMDA has 275 chapters with 45,000 members internationally, and a 57-member scientific advisory board comprised of highly recognized experts in medical fields relating to depressive disorders. This organization is dedicated to providing education, advocacy, and self-help support for patients and their families through their many local chapters.

National Mental Health Association (NMHA)
1021 Prince Street
Alexandria, VA 22314-2971
Telephone: 703-684-7722
Information Center: 1-800-969-NMHA
President and Chief Executive Officer: Michael M. Faenza

Founded in 1909, NMHA is the oldest national mental health advocacy association. It is a voluntary charitable organization with more than 80 years of success in working to change the way America thinks about mental health and mental illness.

The NMHA, with a million members, has a mission as a force for social change through advocacy, education, and alignment with consumer interests and rights. It has chartered organizations in 36 states, with 326 local affiliates serving their communities through self-help and support groups.

NMHA's information center answers hundreds of calls and letters weekly from people requesting information, and it provides brochures and pamphlet series on a variety of mental health topics.

The National Depression Screening Day Project
One Washington Street, Suite 304
Wellesley Hills, MA 02181
Telephone: 617-239-0071

The National Depression Screening Day Project provides free screenings for depression at thousands of sites across the country each October during Mental Illness Awareness Week, and at other times in some locations. Founded by Harvard psychiatrist Dr. Douglas G. Jacobs, the program is sponsored by several major mental health organizations.

You may call for the location of a free depression screening site near you. You can learn more about depression, take a confidential written screening test, and discuss the results with a mental health professional all on the same day. In 1993, 56,000 people took this test nationwide, including nearly 1,500 persons whose depression was sufficiently severe that they were considered to be at risk for suicide.

ORGANIZATIONS FOR PROVIDERS OF MENTAL HEALTH

American Association for Marriage and Family Therapy (AAMFT)
REFERRALS
1100 Seventeenth Street, N.W., 10th Fl.
Washington, DC 20036-4601
Telephone: 1-800-374-2638
Contact: John Hutchins, Public Information

The AAMFT is the professional organization representing more than 16,000 marriage and family therapists in the United States, Canada, and abroad. You can call the toll-free number, or send them a self-addressed stamped envelope to receive a list of clinical members in your zip-code area, along with the "Consumer's Guide to Marriage and Family Therapy." Family therapists work with individuals, couples, and families with an emphasis on looking at family dynamics.

American Association of Pastoral Counselors (AAPC)
9504 A Lee Highway
Fairfax, VA 22031-2303
Telephone: 703-385-6967

The AAPC is an international organization of clergy and other religious-oriented professionals whose ministry is helping persons grow in times of life crisis through the services of counseling and psychotherapy. It was founded in 1963, and its 3,000 members include professional pastoral counselors, community clergy, and other helping professionals. AAPC establishes standards for training and supervision in this field, leading to certification of individuals and accreditation of institutions.

A 1992 Gallup Poll found that when confronted with a personal problem 66 percent of persons would prefer a therapist who represented spiritual values and beliefs, and 81 percent would prefer a therapist who enabled them to integrate their values and belief system into the counseling process. This describes the certified pastoral counselor. Referrals are made to local pastoral counselors.

American Psychiatric Association (APA)
Division of Public Affairs
Dept. P.A.
1400 K Street, N.W.
Washington, DC 20005
Telephone: 202-682-6220
Medical Director: Melvin Sabshin, M.D.

This organization, the oldest specialty society in the country, was established in 1844. Its 38,500 members are physicians who specialize in the diagnosis and treatment of mental illness. For those interested in the services of a psychiatrist, it offers referrals to one of its 76 local psychiatric societies. Psychiatrists are the only mental health professionals who are licensed to provide medication, if that is needed.

American Psychological Association (APA)
750 First Street, N.E.
Washington, DC 20002-4242
APA Public Affairs Office: 1-800-374-3120

The American Psychological Association is the largest scientific and professional organization representing psychology in the

United States and the world's largest association of psychologists. When APA was founded in 1892, psychology was a new profession—today there are over 124,000 members. APA works to advance psychology as a science, as a profession, and as a means of promoting human welfare. Those seeking referrals will be given the numbers of local organizations within their state.

National Association of Social Workers (NASW)
750 First Street N.E., Suite 700
Washington, DC 20002
Telephone: 202-408-8600

The NASW is the national organization and accrediting body for over 150,000 social workers in the United States. Clinical social workers provide more than one-half of all mental health services including both public and private counseling. They are trained to counsel people using a systems approach that includes all areas of personal involvement: community, school, work, social and family life. Referrals to clinical social workers will be made directly and to local chapters who will provide additional resources in your area.

ETHNIC MINORITY PROVIDERS OF MENTAL HEALTH

Asian American Psychological Association (AAPA)
Slippery Rock University
Dept. of Counseling and Educational Psychology
Slippery Rock, PA
Telephone: 412-738-2274
President: Dr. S. Andrew Chen

Founded in 1973, the AAPA seeks to advance the welfare of Asian Americans through the development of psychological theories and practices that reflect ethnic diversity in American society. The association has 300 members including Asian-American psychologists and others who are committed to these concerns. There is an annual journal and a newsletter. Those interested in information or referrals to affiliated therapists can call or write.

Association of Black Psychologists (ABP)
P.O. Box 55999
Washington, DC 20040-5999
Telephone: 202-722-0808
President: Dr. Wade W. Nobles

Founded in 1968, the ABP aims to enhance the psychological well-being of black people, and to develop policies that impact on the mental health of the black community. ABP publishes a journal and a newsletter, and offers a referral network.

Society of Indian Psychologists (SIP)
119 N. Foreman Avenue
Norman, OK 73069
President: Dr. Dolores Subia BigFoot

The SIP is an association of approximately 120 mental health professionals and others involved in issues relating to or affecting Native Americans. The society publishes a newsletter. Interested persons may write for further information.

National Hispanic Psychological Association (NHPA)
Division of Educational Psychology
Arizona State University
Tempe, AZ 85287-0611
Telephone: 602-965-1352
President: Andres Barona, Ph.D.

In existence for over 20 years, the NHPA has over 700 members including psychologists and others who are committed to serving the mental health needs of the Hispanic population. This organization is dedicated to serving both Spanish-speaking and non-Spanish-speaking people, native-born citizens and immigrants from many countries. The NHPA promotes new research, publishes a newsletter, and makes referrals.

ORGANIZATIONS FOR SENIOR CITIZENS

Alzheimer's Association (A.A.)
919 N. Michigan Avenue, Suite 1000
Chicago, IL 60611-1676
Telephone: 312-335-8700; TDD: 312-335-8882

Approximately 4 million Americans have Alzheimer's disease, and 14 million will suffer from this condition by the middle of the twenty-first century unless a cure or prevention is found. The Alzheimer's Association is the oldest and largest national voluntary health organization dedicated to research for the causes, cure, and prevention of Alzheimer's and related disorders. It provides education and support services to patients, their families, and caregivers. Call or write for further information.

Alzheimer's Disease Education and Referral Center (ADEAR)
P.O. Box 8250
Silver Spring, MD 20907-8250
Telephone: 301-495-3311
           800-438-4380

A service of the National Institute on Aging, ADEAR distributes information on Alzheimer's disease, on current research, activities, and services available to patients and their families. They will respond to written and phone inquiries, and they will provide referrals to key state, regional, and national resources.

American Association for Retired Persons (AARP)
601 E Street, N.W.
Washington, DC 20049
Telephone: 202-434-2560

AARP is the nation's oldest and largest organization for people age 50 and older, with more than 33 million members, one-third of whom are still in the workforce. AARP serves their needs and interests through legislative advocacy, research, informative programs, and community services provided by a network of local chapters and experienced volunteers throughout the country. The organization also offers members a wide range of discounts and special benefits, including *Modern Maturity* magazine and the monthly *Bulletin*.

National Institute on Aging—Information Center (NIA-IC)
P.O. Box 8057
Gaithersburg, MD 20898-8057
Telephone: 301-587-2528
           800-222-2225; TDD 800-222-4225

The National Institute on Aging—Information Center is the publication distribution and information arm of NIA. The NIA-IC operates a toll-free service as part of its education program for the general public, mass media, physicians, health-care workers, other government agencies, and service organizations. Publications on a wide variety of topics on health and aging are available free of charge.

FINANCIAL PROBLEMS: DEBT
AND COMPULSIVE SPENDING

Consumer Credit Counseling Service (CCCS)
Affiliated with The National Foundation for Consumer Credit
** (NFCC)**
Telephone: 1-800-338-CCCS (2227)

Debt problems frequently develop over a period of time and consumers are often unaware they are in serious trouble until it's too late. The NFCC serves as the umbrella group for more than 1,100 Consumer Credit Counseling Service offices in the United States, Canada, and Puerto Rico. The NFCC is a nonprofit membership organization whose purpose is to educate, counsel, and promote the wise use of credit.

CCCS offices are nonprofit and offer free or low-cost professional financial guidance and budget counseling to consumers across the country. These services may include individually designed debt repayment programs. The CCCS offices never turn away consumers because of an inability to pay. To contact the CCCS office nearest you, locate the telephone number in the business pages of your local directory or call the toll-free number. In 1993 CCCS offices counseled 645,700 families. You do not have to be in serious debt to use their services.

Debtors Anonymous (DA)
P.O. Box 400, Grand Central Station
New York, NY 10163-0400
Telephone: 212-642-8220

Debtors Anonymous is a 12-step program for mutual help in recovering from compulsive indebtedness. The primary purpose is to help group members to stay solvent and to help other compulsive debtors to achieve solvency. Founded in 1976, this is an affiliation of over 400 local groups. They maintain a newsletter and phone support network. Write or call for information about groups in your area or look in your local Yellow Page directory.

HOTLINES

AIDS

National AIDS Hotlines
Telephone: 1-800-342-AIDS (24-hour hotline, 7 days)
              1-800-344-SIDA (Spanish; 8 a.m.–2 a.m., 7 days)
              1-800-AIDS-TTY (TDD) (10 a.m.–10 p.m. Mon-Fri.)

These toll-free numbers provide free information, referral and literature about AIDS. These hotlines are funded and supported by the Center for Disease Control. All calls are handled discreetly and confidentially.

SUBSTANCE ABUSE

Center for Substance Abuse Treatment (CSAT)
National Drug Information, Treatment, and Referral Hotline
Telephone: 1-800-662-HELP English
              1-800-66-AYUDA Spanish
              1-800-228-0427 TDD Hearing Impaired

CSAT provides information on alcohol/drug abuse and on HIV/AIDS as it relates to substance abuse. It offers referrals to drug and alcohol treatment programs and to self-help groups. The Hotline is a caring, confidential service that is available to all 50 states and U.S. Territories.

Operational Hours: 9 a.m. to 3 a.m. (E.S.T.) Monday–Friday; 12 p.m. to 3 a.m. (E.S.T.) Saturday–Sunday

The Hotline's primary mission is to provide referrals for drug users or family members to treatment resources. (Requests for printed literature should be addressed to the National Clearing House of Alcoholism and Drug Information—NCADI; their telephone number is 1-800-729-6686.)

CHILD ABUSE/FAMILY VIOLENCE

The Childhelp/National Child Abuse Hotline
Telephone: 1-800-422-4453
              1-800-4-A-CHILD
              1-800-2-A-CHILD (TDD)

This service is available 24 hours a day to intervene in crisis situations and to provide specific information and local referrals if you or someone you know needs help. This hotline is available in many languages.

The National Council on Child Abuse and Family Violence
1155 Connecticut Ave., N.W., Suite 400
Washington, DC 20036
Telephone: 1-800-222-2000

This is 24 hour hotline providing information and referral on child abuse and other family violence: For spouse and partner abuse (1-800-537-2238), and for elder abuse (1-800-879-6682).

YOUTH IN CRISIS: National Runaway Switchboard
Telephone: 1-800-621-4000

This is a 24 hour hotline for information and referral for young people requiring shelter, counseling, food, transportation, and suicide and crisis counseling.

National Runaway Hotline
1-800-HOT-HOME

This is another 24 hour crisis counseling service for runaways, and youth with other problems, and parents.

SUICIDE HOTLINE

In case of emergency you can always call 911 or your local hospital, clinic, or emergency room, or the local police.

The Alpine Helpline
17800 Woodruff
P.O. Box 1064
Bellflower, CA 90706
Telephone: 1-800-877-7675

The Alpine Helpline is a national crisis, suicide, and referral line that provides information and referrals for the treatment of mental health and substance abuse problems. A privately funded organization, they provide this live service free of charge from 6 a.m. to 11 p.m. P.S.T.

ALCOHOL

National Alcohol and Drug Abuse Hotline
Telephone: 1-800-Alcohol or 1-800-252-6465

This is a 24 hour information and referral hotline for all chemical dependency problems.

The National Council on Alcohol & Drugs
Telephone: 1-800-475-Hope

This is another 24 hour hotline which will provide information and connect callers to local treatment centers.

SELF-HELP GROUPS (12 Step Groups)

Alcoholics Anonymous (A.A.)
General Service Office
A.A. World Services, Inc.
475 Riverside Drive, 11th Floor
New York, NY 10015
Telephone: 212-870-3400

Founded in 1935, this is an international network of over 94,000 groups. The emphasis is on sharing experience, strength, and hope with others so that members may solve their common problems and achieve sobriety. A.A.'s sole purpose is to help the alcoholic recover through the 12-step program. Call or write for information.

Al-Anon Family Groups
P.O. Box 862
Midtown Station
New York, NY 10018-6106
Telephone: 212-302-7240 or 800-344-2666 (re: meetings)
800-356-9996 (re: general)

Founded in 1951, this is an international network of over 32,000 groups. This is a fellowship of men, women, children, and adult children whose lives have been affected by the compulsive drinking of a family member or friend. Al-Anon follows the 12 steps adopted from A.A. Call or write for guidelines for starting groups, or for literature available in 29 languages.

Adult Children of Alcoholics—World Service Organization (ACA)
P.O. Box 3216
Torrance, CA 90510
Telephone: 310-534-1815

Founded in 1976, ACA is an international network of over 1,800 groups. This is a 12-step program of discovery and recovery for adults who realize that the characteristics that allowed them to survive as children in an alcoholic dysfunctional home now prevent them from fully experiencing life.

Co-Dependents Anonymous (CODA)
P.O. Box 33577
Phoenix, AZ 85067-3577
Telephone: 602-277-7991

Founded in 1986, CODA is an international network of 3,500 groups. This is a fellowship of men, women, and teenagers whose common problem is an inability to maintain functional relationships. Members desire healthy, fulfilling relationships with others and with themselves. CODA follows the 12-step program adapted from A.A. Call or write for newsletter, literature, and audio tapes.

Emotions Anonymous (EA)
P.O. Box 4245
St. Paul, MN 55104
Telephone: 612-647-9712

Founded in 1971, EA is a national network of 1,200 chapters. It is a fellowship of men and women sharing experiences, hopes, and strengths with each other, using a 12-step program, in order to gain better emotional health. Call or write for information or newsletter.

Gamblers Anonymous (GA)
P.O. Box 17173
Los Angeles, CA 90017
Telephone: 213-386-8789

Founded in 1957, GA is an international network of 1,200 chapters. This is a fellowship of men and women who share experiences, strength, and hope with each other to recover from compulsive gambling, following a 12-step program. Call or write for monthly bulletin and chapter development kit.

Narcotics Anonymous (NA)
P.O. Box 9999
Van Nuys, CA 91409
Telephone: 818-780-3951

Founded in 1953, this an international network of over 22,000 groups. This is a fellowship of men and women for whom drugs had become a major problem. Recovering addicts meet regularly to help each other stay clean and sober. Call or write for monthly magazine, pen pal program, group development guidelines, literature in braille and 7 languages, and audio tapes.

Overeaters Anonymous (OA)
P.O. Box 92870
Los Angeles, CA 90009
Telephone: 310-618-8835

Founded in 1960, OA is an international network of 9,968 groups. This 12-step fellowship meets to help one another understand and overcome compulsive eating disorders. There are also groups and literature for young persons and teenagers. Call or write for monthly magazine, bi-monthly newsletter, and group development guidelines.

Sex and Love Addicts Anonymous (Augustine Fellowship-SLAA)
P.O. Box 119
New Town Branch
Boston, MA 02258
Telephone: 617-332-1845

Founded in 1976, this is an international network of 1,000 affiliated groups. This is a 12-step fellowship based on A.A. for those who desire to stop living out a pattern of sex and love addiction, obsessive/compulsive sexual behavior or emotional attachment. Call or write for newsletter, journal, phone support, information, and referrals.

OTHER SELF-HELP GROUPS

Rational Recovery
P.O. Box 800
Lotus, CA 95651
Telephone: 916-621-4374

Founded in 1986, Rational Recovery has an international network of over 350 groups. Its purpose is to help individuals achieve recovery from substance abuse and addictive behavior through self-reliance and self-help groups. Unlike most recovery groups it is strictly non-religious and its principles are based on rational emotive therapy. Call or write for information, newsletter, and referrals.

Recovery, Inc.
International Headquarters
802 N. Dearborn Street
Chicago, IL 60610
Telephone: 312-337-5661

Recovery, Inc. is a community mental health organization that offers systematic training in a self-help method for controlling temperamental behavior and handling anxiety, anger, depression, and fears. (This method is also referred to as cognitive behavior therapy.)

Recovery, Inc. was established in 1937 by the late psychiatrist, Abraham A. Low, M.D. Meetings are open to anyone, there is no required fee although a voluntary contribution is suggested. Recovery, Inc. has been honored as one of the true, original pioneers in the field of self-help. In an era of escalating costs, Recovery, Inc. is unique in offering an inexpensive, time-tested, systematic method of self-help. This organization has helped literally tens of thousands of people to lead normal lives. It faithfully delivers a low-cost adjunct to professional care. People seeking help will be referred to local groups.

Notes

1. Adapted from The Holmes and Rahe Social Re-adjustment Rating Scale, *Journal of Psychosomatic Research,* Vol. 11, pp. 213–18. Copyright Pergamon Press, 1967.

2. Adapted by National Depression Screening Project director, Dr. Douglas Jacobs, from the Zung Self-Rating Depression Scale. Copyright Dr. William Zung, 1965, 1974. All rights reserved. Reproduced with permission of the author's family.

3. Adapted from American Psychiatric Association brochure, "Let's Talk Facts About—Mental Health of the Elderly," 1992.

4. Adapted from "The Measurement of Life Satisfaction," by Neugarten, Bernice, L., Havighurst, Robert J., and Tobin, Sheldon S. *Journal of Gerontology,* Vol. 16, No. 2, April 1961, pp. 134–43; and "Analysis of a Life Satisfaction Index," by David L. Adams, *Journal of Gerontology,* Vol. 24, No. 4, pp. 470–74.

5. Adapted from American Psychiatric Association brochure, "Let's Talk Facts About—Alzheimer's Disease," 1992.

6. *Ibid.*

7. *Ibid.*

8. Adapted from two articles on preventing senility and Alzheimers: "Building a Better Brain," by Daniel Golden and Alexander Tsiaras, *Life* magazine, July 1994, p. 62–70. "Use It or Lose It," by Paul McCarthy, *Omni* magazine, February 1994, p. 34.

9. Adapted from American Association for Marriage and Family Therapy brochure, "A Consumer's Guide to Marriage and Family Therapy," 1991.

10. "Reaching for the Light: A Resource Guide For Coping with Mental Health Problems." The Mental Health Association of California, Sacramento, 1992.

11. Statistics compiled from National Institute of Mental Health, *Health Care Reform for Americans with Severe Mental Illnesses: Report of the National Advisory Mental Health Council,* March, 1993; and U.S. Congress Office of Technology and Assessment, *The Biology of Mental Disorders,* Government Printing Office, September 1992.

Bibliography

Aging and Alzheimer's

Friedan, Betty. *The Foundation of Age.* Simon and Schuster, 1993. (A fascinating personal account, investigating our society's basic attitudes toward aging, with supporting research).

Mace, Nancy and Rabina, Peter. *The 36-Hour Day: A Family Guide to Caring for Persons with Alzheimer's Disease and Related Dementing Illnesses.* Johns Hopkins University Press, 1991. (Another very good, popular family guide to home care for patients with dementing illnesses.)

Powell, Leonore and Courtice, Katie. *Alzheimer's Disease—A Guide for Families.* Addison-Wesley, 1983. (A useful and practical aid for families coping with Alzheimer's).

Anxiety

Beck, Aaron. *Anxieties and Phobias.* Basic Books, 1983. (A basic understanding of anxieties and phobias and how to manage them.)

Ross, Jerilyn. *Triumph Over Fear: A Book of Help and Hope for People with Anxiety, Panic Attacks and Phobias.* Bantam Books, 1994. (A very practical guidebook offering effective coping strategies for people with these problems.)

Coping Strategies for Families with Mental Illness

Hatfield, Agnes. *Coping with Mental Illness in the Family: A Family Guide.* Published by and purchased from National Association for Mental Illness, NAMI Book #6. (A useful handbook for families dealing with these challenges; if interested call 703-524-7600.)

Woolis, Rebecca. *When Someone You Love Has Mental Illness.* Tarcher/Perigee, 1992. (Practical, comprehensive, and clearly written for families recently stricken with severe mental illness.)

Depression, Manic-Depression and Mood Disorders

De Paulo, Raymond, Jr. and Ablow, Keith. *How to Cope with Depression.* Ballentine Books, 1989. (This book considers depression from the perspectives of disease, personality, and behavior, and explains recent findings on causes and treatments of mood disorders.)

Dowling, Colette. *You Mean I Don't Have to Feel This Way.* Bantam Books, 1993. (A personal account focusing on the biochemical causes, treatments, and interrelationships of depressive illness, eating disorders, anxiety panic attacks, alcoholism, and addictions.)

Duke, Patty and Hockman, Gloria. *A Brilliant Madness: Living with Manic-Depressive Illness.* Bantam Books, 1992. (Ms. Duke's insights and frank descriptions of the effect of manic-depression on her life, supplemented by relevant medical information.)

Fieve, Ronald. *Moodswing.* William Morrow and Company, 1989. (A medical pioneer discusses the use of lithium, and the latest antidepressant drugs, when hospitalization is necessary, and teenage and adult suicide.)

Greist, John and Jefferson, James. *Depression and Its Treatment.* American Psychiatric Press, 1992. (A straightforward and concise guide answering basic questions about depression. Effectiveness and side-effects of conventional treatments are discussed, and other approaches.)

Klein, Donald F. and Wender, Paul. *Understanding Depression: A Complete Guide to its Diagnosis and Treatment.* Oxford University Press, 1993. (This short, easy to read paperback provides basic information about diagnosis and treatment of depressive illnesses, including manic-depression.)

Financial Assistance

Bradshaw, John. *Healing the Shame that Binds You*. Health Communications, 1988. (An emotional and revealing discussion of how shame is a core problem in human compulsions and addictions; and techniques for healing shame.)

Mooney, Al and Eisenberg, Howard and Arlene. *The Recovery Book*. Workman Publishing, 1992. (An excellent, and comprehensive book about literally everything related to recovering alcoholics and addicts.)

Mundis, Jerrold. *How to Get Out of Debt, Stay Out of Debt and Live Prosperously*. Bantam Books, 1988. (Negotiating with creditors, collection agencies, and the IRS—the tried and proven ways of Debtors Anonymous.)

Whitfield, Charles. *Healing the Child Within*. Health Communications, 1987. (Discovery and recovery for adult children of dysfunctional families—a highly readable and clear guidebook.)

Stress

Selye, Hans. *The Stress of Life*. McGraw Hill, 1978. (A classic book about the basics of human stress, adaptation and patterns of physiological response by a famous researcher.)

General

Bloomfield, Harold. *Making Peace with Your Parents: The Key to Enriching Your Life and All Your Relationships*. Ballantine Books, 1985. (A practical guide for improving relationships that includes valuable exercises and personal growth techniques.)

Bruno, Frank. *Psychological Symptoms*. John Wiley and Sons, 1993. (A valuable reference for common mental and emotional problems, and how to cope with them.)

Burns, David. *Feeling Good: The New Mood Therapy*. William Morrow and Co., 1980. (A pioneering book that introduces the principles of cognitive therapy—a useful and systematic approach to overcoming depression and other problems.)

Ellis, Albert. *A New Guide to Rational Living*. Prentice Hall, 1975. (Another classic in the field of rational emotive psychotherapy—a behavioral approach to improving your life.)

Frankl, Victor. *Man's Search for Meaning*. Simon and Schuster, 1984. (A classic describing the principles of logotherapy—a very personal account from a holocaust survivor.)

Glasser, William. *Reality Therapy: A New Approach to Psychiatry.* Harper Collins, 1975. (A time-tested book in the field of rational-emotive therapy—tried and true strategies for dealing with problems in the here and now.)

Missildine, Hugh. *Your Inner Child of the Past.* Pocket Books, Simon & Schuster, 1982. (A very popular book that describes the childhood roots and basic sources of emotional problems in adult life.)

Reaching for the Light: A Resource Guide for Coping with Mental Health Problems, Mental Health Association in Sacramento, California, free booklet can be ordered directly: 916-441-4627. (An excellent, brief introduction to all aspects of finding a therapist and going for help.)

Index

226   *Index*